THE

NFT

REVOLUTION 2021

- 2 in 1 -

BASIC GUIDE FOR BEGINNERS + CRYPTO ART & REAL ESTATE EDITION

Create, Buy, Sell And Make a Profit With Non-Fungible Tokens

CRYPTO DUKEDOM

First edition: May 2021.

Published by CRYPTO DUKEDOM

TABLE OF CONTENTS

BASIC GUIDE

Introduction .... pg. 08
1. Brief history .... pg. 12
2. Nft & key concepts .... pg. 15
3. Nft & blockchain .... pg. 26
4. Discovering nfts .... pg. 32
5. Smart contracts .... pg. 37
6. Digital assets .... pg. 43
7. Nft – areas & uses .... pg. 45
8. How to create, buy and sell nfts .... pg. 54
9. 10 disruptive projects .... pg. 61
10. Nft – pros, cons and the future .... pg. 64

CRYPTO ART REVOLUTION

11. Crypto art vs tradional art market .... pg. 70
12. Crypto art: an overview .... pg. 74
13. Crypto art: brief history .... pg. 78
14. Crypto art: 14 key features .... pg. 80
15. Opportunities and risks .... pg. 87
16. How to become a crypto artist .... pg. 89
17. Best crypto art ideas .... pg. 93
18. How to sell crypto art .... pg. 95
19. Top marketplaces .... pg. 99
20. How to buy and invest .... pg. 104
21. Success stories .... pg. 109
22. Best innovative artists and their projects .. pg. 113

NFT AND REAL ESTATE

23. Nft and real estate .... pg. 119
24. Nft & real estate: that's amazing news! .....pg. 127
25. Nft & real estate – disruptive projects ...... pg. 142

ABOUT US .... pg. 166

INTRODUCTION

"The technology is real. The impact is real and permanent." That's a statement from billionaire investor and NBA franchise owner Mark Cuban, who is at the forefront of the explosion of interest in blockchain and non-fungible token technology. According to Cuban, the impact of this monetary technological shift is measurable and lasting. Once stabilized, it will disrupt how money is invested, collected, played with, and made.

Whether it's sports, entertainment, gaming, art, music, or fashion, non-fungible tokens are a perfect fit for any industry or field. This revolutionary technology has been talked about increasingly in the past few months, but not everyone knows about it yet, and its potential has not yet been fully imagined.

Non-fungible tokens, more simply called NFTs, are a unique digital resource. Indeed, what the non-fungible token creates is a verifiable digital scarcity, which results in unique value.

Those who already understand a bit about blockchain, cryptocurrencies, and tokens know what we are talking about and will be able to untangle this type of technology better. In simple words, you could say that a fungible token consists of digital information recorded in a blockchain that grants the object a particular right that is recognizable as ownership. Tokens are, in essence, a certificate of authenticity, while "fungible" refers to the replicability and interchangeability of cryptocurrencies such as Bitcoin, the cryptocurrency created in 2009, or even a fiat currency (dollar, euro, pound, etc.). Non-fungible tokens are distinguishable precisely by their non-fungibility—that is, their non-interchangeability. They are able to provide a unique representation of a virtual asset and are authentic, unique, and encrypted.

An image in a .jpg file, for example, can be replicated countless times, but the token cannot be, and it is the token itself that gives value to the image, enabling it to bought, sold, and collected like the finest works of art. Therefore, the purchased token is a certification of the media or digital work, not the work itself. NFTs, consequently, give a digital creation all the rights it would have as a physical work: rarity, authenticity, and ownership. That's what makes an NFT so extraordinary. Non-fungible tokens are changing the digital world forever. It's a bit like an artist creating a work of art for just one person: many might admire it on the web and appreciate its beauty, but only the person who buys it holds the rights of ownership, including the ability to resell it and make a profit.

Talking about NFT is a bit like referring to a parallel universe that is growing exponentially. Indeed, recent depictions of NFT use words like "mania" and "bubble" to describe the situation.

In 2020, the trading volume of the NFT market exceeded $250 million, a four-fold increase over 2019, and they are continuing to grow by the minute even at the time of this writing. It's a world that has quickly garnered the attention of celebrities, international artists, sports figures, digital creatives, entrepreneurs, influencers, and many more.

Several striking cases have made their way around the web. For instance, it's hard not to have heard of how the NBA's NFT platform, NBA Top Shot, sold a clip of Lebron James' formidable dunk for$ 208k or how Lindsay Lohan sold a photo of herself for +$50k dollars and donated the proceeds to charity. The same celebrities who have taken an interest in non-fungible tokens have brought them into the limelight by making them mainstream and grossing record amounts. Besides, NFTs can be found in virtually every industry, from business and social media to music, art, sports, and entertainment.

The exclusivity of digital files has resulted in them selling for millions of dollars. Following the granular price tiering principle, an artist sells their most exclusive works at higher prices and subsequent works at lower prices. Moreover, NFTs are so great precisely because of their ability to remove all intermediation: artist and buyer are in direct contact in a whole new way.

Grimes, famous synth-pop star, singer, and girlfriend of well-known entrepreneur Elon Musk, earned $5.8 million in less than 20 minutes by selling her NFTs on Nifty Gateway, one of the most popular marketplaces. The collection was titled War Nymph. It features winged children sporting javelins, tattoos, and elf ears in a dystopian world. The singer first announced the auction of her NFTs in a tweet, writing simply: "Enter the void." With respect to this digital world, she declared: "The digital realm makes the realm more rare and precious. It also offers escapism and perfection. Sometimes I want imperfection, real life. Sometimes I want perfection."

Like her and also in the music business, Kings of Leon recently got into the craze. They released their album *When You See Yourself* as an NFT on the Yellowheart platform. The album is available to everyone in traditional formats, but those in NFT were sold for $50, each offering different perks: digital downloads, concert tickets, and a limited-edition vinyl copy of the album. In this way, digital becomes physical and vice versa, creating a unique and original offering.

Just over a year ago, Twitter founder and CEO Jack Dorsey also auctioned off the NFT of his first tweet from 2006 in which he declared "Just setting up my twitter." It sold for $2.9 million, and he donated the proceeds to charity. The platform on which he sold his NFT is Valuables by Cent. If even the tech enthusiast and founder of a platform as popular as Twitter has entered the world of NFT auctions, we can assume there's some potential there.

The most glaring case in point? Beeple, a digital graphic designer originally from South Carolina, kick-started a real crypto art movement by selling his work titled *The First 5000* days for $69.3 million, the highest quote ever achieved by a digital artist. The famous art auction house Christie's is relying on MakersPlace to support the new digital trend, seeing great opportunities for a world of art in which even the younger generations, accustomed to digital creations, can invest.

How does an intangible good that everyone can see reach such a value? How and who can create and sell their works in NFT? What applications and results can they generate in the future? Is this a stable market in which to invest?

In this guide, we will answer these and other similar questions as we provide a detailed introduction to and analysis of non-fungible tokens: what they are, how they are created, what is their market, what are there possible uses, opportunities, merits, and demerits, and more, including famous collections and artists as well as case studies of a phenomenon that is as revolutionary as it is recent.

The possibilities of selling, collecting, investing, and earning are what make non-fungible tokens a compelling technological opportunity. Moreover, this opportunity will not be extinguished, as it is likely to find more and more markets and uses. So, without further ado, let's begin our clear, simple, thorough, and beginner-proof analysis of NFTs.

BRIEF HISTORY

Although the success of NFTs has exploded relatively recently (thanks largely to the record $69.3 million sale of the digital artwork by artist Beeple, stage name Mike Winkelmann, which was hammered out by Christie's auction house at 4 p.m. on March 11, 2021), NFT is not a new technology. Following the emergence of Bitcoins, projects have sprung up that take advantage of the particular internal protocol of the Bitcoin blockchain. By closely monitoring the origin of a given bitcoin, a set of coins can be colored to distinguish it from the rest. These coins can then have special properties and a value independent of the bitcoins' face value. The use of these protocols has generated tokens that have been called "colored coins." These colored coins, born around 2012-2013, were actually the first NFTs in history.

The functioning of colored coins was not very different from non-fungible tokens as we know them: their purpose is to represent a multitude of resources within metadata. The main reason why colored coins were invented is to open the door to develop new features in Bitcoin. The ability to create tokens linked to things in the real world and for these to be supported by a blockchain network presented a unique opportunity. Colored coins used the transaction model called Genesis and paved the way for new experimentation, especially in terms of placing real-world assets on distributed ledgers.

In 2014, Counterparty, an open-source platform where peer-to-peer applications can be developed, was born. Initially, these applications were oriented to the financial sector on the Bitcoin blockchain. Currently, the protocol implements and supports the creation of assets, the issuance of bonds from these assets, and the trading of assets using a decentralized market. Its open-source protocol allows you to write smart contracts, turning many real world actions into a code that works automatically without the need for intermediaries and is very secure.

Counterparty was born precisely because of the desire to develop all the resources related to blockchain and enabled by colored coins. The founders, Robert Dermody, Adam Krellenstein, and Evan Wagner, based everything on a token called XCP. Counterparty's idea became very famous in 2014, resulting in the first blockchain-based game ever created, Sells of Genesis, and trading card games like Force of Will being invented the following year. After that, memes moved into the blockchain sphere, specifically in 2016 with "Rare Pepes" which are images of Pepe the Frog, the green anthropomorphic frog with a humanoid body from Matt Furie's comic book *Boy's Club*. This moment seemed to open the doors for people to see the possibility of developing a substantial market around unique digital pieces.

The decisive year for the birth of the first NFTs was 2017, when Ethereum began to gain importance, first by announcing its own collection of unique Pepe or Peperium memes and then, definitively, with Cryptopunks.

The breakthrough occurred when John Watkinson and Matt Hall realized that they could create unique characters generated on Ethereum's blockchain. The characters were limited versions, and no two characters were the same. This was the birth of the CryptoPunks project.

Watkinson and Hall decided to allow anyone with an Ethereum wallet to claim a Cryptopunk for free, and so it happened that the characters were all claimed. Following their success, the first blockchain-based virtual game that allows players to adopt, breed, and trade virtual cats was also born. It's called

Cryptokitties and is perfect for those who loved to dabble with Tamagotchi in the 90s.

This project soon went viral and made headlines in major media outlets because people were making insane profits by selling digital kittens for as much as $100,000. Soon after, creators of Cryptokitties developed the company Dapper Labs, increasing business and interested investors even more.

Today, there are a lot of projects out there based on NFTs. For example, thanks to the virtual wallet Metamask (among the most popular), you can import your virtual coins and change them in Ethereum, the currency (cryptocurrency) of NFT. After that, you can buy tokens from the most flourishing markets and through different marketplaces, of which the most famous is OpenSea. Ethereum's platform is based on various technical standards for different types of tokens that allow interactions to work properly. The most common standard is ERC20, where ERC stands for Ethereum Request for Comment. Today, NFTs are based on the ERC721 standard, which was invented specifically to track the movements and properties of individual tokens and allow them to be recognized.

The history of NFTs is recent and winding, and recognizing the multitude of projects and enormous turnover, we can safely assume that growth will be exponential. Investments in unique digital products are increasingly rapidly. Collectors have made it a real craze. The market is increasing its reach by implementing NFTs that correspond to the needs of buyers who can enjoy the returns of their investments.

NFT - KEY CONCEPTS

N FTs have reached such a level of fame not only due to the celebrities who participated in creating, buying, and selling them, but also due to something intrinsic to NFTs themselves: their ability to create value. To fully understand what NFTs are, you don't just need to know about the technology they are based on; you need to understand a few key concepts. This knowledge will reveal the beauty of NFTs, and you will be amazed at their impact on everyone's lives and their future direction.

To better understand the topic, we will try to start with the basics and review each essential term thoroughly.

OBJECTIVE VALUE VERSUS SUBJECTIVE VALUE

People attach value to many things, including objects, activities, goals, careers, and more. If you were to ask a group of people what a valuable experience or thing is to them, you would receive a wide range of answers, perhaps including a luxury sports car, a nice walk on a dream beach, being with friends, listening to good music, etc. The common thread that runs through these items is desire. What tends to be considered valuable is thought of that way because of the intrinsic desire that is felt in achieving or satisfying it. We don't desire objects, experiences, or anything else because of the feeling these create but because of the desire they satisfy. And desire creates subjective value.

The concept of value is intimately tied to preferences, which tend to be arbitrary and depend on what a given person believes, desires, or perceives. Through desires, the reasons for pursuing pleasure are perpetuated. Moreover, the more desires are satisfied, the more value is produced. Subjective value, therefore, is the value that each individual is willing to assign to a good. Thus, it is arbitrary and temporary. Try to think about it: an urgent necessity can increase the value of a good exponentially with respect to what might be considered normal or average.

Trying to define objective value is not as simple. Although we can speak of the temporary and not arbitrary objectivity of prices (where the price of a good is not fixed by a central power), there is no reasonable way to determine value objectively. Thus, where not established in a coercive manner by an authority, all value is exclusively subjective: the market price is generated by subjective evaluations.

Therefore, the value is not something intrinsic to the product. It is not one of its properties, but simply the importance that we attribute to the satisfaction of our needs in relation to our life and our well-being.

THE MARKET

The correlation between subjective value and market prices is one of the most imperceptible aspects of modern economics. It is the correlation between subjective value and objective monetary prices. When referring to subjective value, there is no single unit of measurement.

Through the attribution of value, people estimate and classify goods according to their preference. The concept of value creation plays a central role in management theory.

The term "marketplace" has two possible meanings. First, it is a physical place where people go to sell, buy, or trade a product or good—for example, a supermarket, a shopping mall, or a car dealership; it can also be digital, including platforms such as Amazon, eBay, Alibaba, Shopify, and many others. Second, the term "market" or "marketplace" can also describe the existence of people who desire to buy, sell, or exchange a certain type of product. There is a market in the sense that there is a certain product that can be elicit desire and be adjusted to consumers' tastes or preferences.

A market is organized according to the following different approaches:

➢ Free competition occurs when the price is formed by the encounter between goods or services offered by competing firms and consumers have the freedom to choose between different offers.
➢ Oligopoly occurs when the offer is made by a small number of operators.
➢ Monopoly: occurs when there is no choice but to accept the price imposed by the offer.

The advent of the free market has produced many benefits for community life. Consumers' needs and the value they place on goods or services are always brought to the forefront within market research and marketing. This understanding of the term is much more abstract: a market exists when there are many people who have an interest in buying or selling a particular product, service, information, or currency.

For all physical assets, the market value is determined by supply and demand and, therefore, by the relationship between the quantity of goods available and the demand. For example, an asset that is highly sought after but scarce acquires value due to the competition between those who want it, while an asset that is available in large quantities or unlimited, even if highly sought after, does not acquire value because those who seek to possess it can easily obtain it. In physical assets, we talk about the concept of scarcity of assets, which has not been part of the digital world for a long time.

A market test is the tool that companies use to identify the types of people who may be interested in a product that is about to be put on the market. This test helps companies to determine how much money people are willing to spend to get their products. The results show that different people are interested in different types of products and that some are willing to spend a specific amount on a specific type of product. Today's companies listen to the needs of consumers and respond to them. Classical economics has always been based on scarcity, which often defines prices and focuses on those products that satisfy 80% of the population. Thanks to the internet, the possibilities have increased exponentially. Whe web offers greater market possibilities because it reaches a global audience, meaning that practically every product or good finds its market of reference. This was Chris Anderson dream with "the long tail" strategy, which is a retail strategy based on statistical analysis in which it os preferred to sell a large number of unique items in relatively small quantities rather than a small number of popular items in large quantities.

The web market is very often devoid of intermediaries. Thus, trust and word-of-mouth opinions are of extreme importance and represent the most current marketing methods online.

FUNGIBLE VERSUS NON-FUNGIBLE ASSETS

To better understand the difference between fungible and non-fungible, it is important to learn about (or brush up on) the concepts of assets, tokens, tokenization, and blockchain.

What is an asset?

Asset is a term used in finance that refers to anything that can be assigned a monetary value and can be useful or desirable. It can be something physical, digital, abstract, or that helps generate earnings. A fungible asset is interchangeable because it possesses the same value as another fungible asset. For example, a bitcoin is a fungible asset because one bitcoin has exactly the same value as another bitcoin. Fungibility is a desirable property for a currency because it allows there to be free exchange when there is no way to know the history of each individual unit. However, fungibility is not a useful property with regard to collectibles.

A non-fungible asset is something that is not interchangeable or even divisible. A non-fungible asset is, for example, a house, a used car, or a unique football card. These cannot be divided because they would not have the same value. A token is nothing more than the digital representation of an asset, which can be anything, as long as it has recognizable and certifiable properties.

In the world of blockchain technology, a token is a virtual token whose value is issued by an organization. Tokens are units of value; they are the representation of a digital asset (a cryptocurrency, a physical product or object, etc.).

In a broad sense, a token is an object with a certain value only within a specific context.

How about an example? Casino chips. These chips are just pieces of plastic that are worth nothing outside the walls of the casino. It is in this context that their value is agreed upon and they become the representation of an asset.

Historically, tokens have been tokens that create coins with value within a given context.

Therefore, the value of a token is what its creator decides to give it. The moment when a token is assigned that property and value is called tokenization and occurs within blockchain technology. The blockchain is a technology that can be equated to a database that collects classified data within computers and networks. Blockchain technology is supported by three pillars: decentralization, transparency, and immutability. Blockchain allows for a decentralized model in which one computer does not have control over the entire network. A decentralized system allows for greater transparency: every movement is recorded within blockchain, and everyone can control the log of movements and transactions. It is almost impossible in physical reality to find a model with such a level of transparency, where everything is recorded and can be seen by everyone. Moreover, this data cannot be altered in any way, and, for this reason, it is immutable.

The tokenization of a digital asset within blockchain technology can create a non-fungible token: an NFT is the unique representation of a real or digital asset that cannot be exchanged for an equivalent because an equivalent does not exist. There is no NFT equal to another in the world. What people can accomplish with NFTs is endless, and the application possibilities cover all sectors, including art, online gaming, music, collectibles of various kinds, exclusive luxury goods, virtual properties, and much more. Blockchain technology adds unique properties to digital assets by providing people with ownership and management of that token and the ability to transfer it to a decentralized, transparent, and immutable platform.

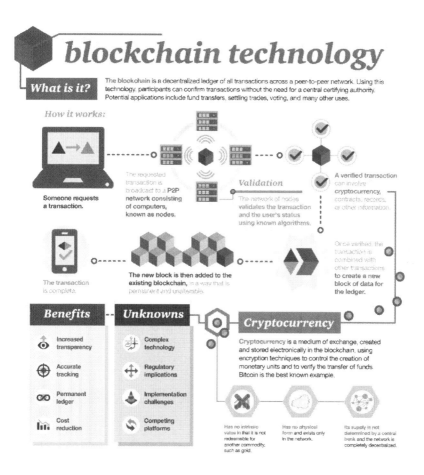

WHAT IS BLOCKCHAIN?

Blockchain is a shared and immutable data chain structure. It is a digital ledger containing data grouped into blocks concatenated together in chronological order whose integrity and credibility is ensured by the use of cryptography. Moreover, once inside it, the content cannot be modified or deleted unless the entire structure is invalidated. This technology is included in the family of distributed ledgers. The blockchain system is distributed across multiple nodes, and there is no single control center. Every transaction is thus recorded. This reinforces the integrity of the process itself. The whole thing is based on a set of properties that represents the foundation of the entire system and that can be defined as the three fundamental pillars of the Blockchain:

1. Decentralization offers the possibility of transferring assets without a unified administration; for example, it allows for the transfer of money without the intervention of a banking institution. Power, within a distributed system, does not lie solely with a single authority. In the blockchain, there are no intermediaries between actions.
2. Transparency allows people to see how simple and secure the system is. Anyone can view transactions on the blockchain but not individual data. This allows for a clear system that allows owners to control their data and all associated movements. In this way, users' privacy is absolutely protected.
3. Immutability can be defined as the ability of a blockchain to remain unchanged and unalterable. No data can be modified, and the database cannot be manipulated in any way because each block is uniquely identified by a value called a hash.

HOW BLOCKCHAIN WORKS

We're used to thinking of blockchain as the core technology of Bitcoin, but blockchain has many other possibilities. Blockchain is not just one thing; it is the abbreviation for an entire suite of distributed technologies capable of recording any type of valuable content, such as financial transactions, medical records, and land holdings. Although we already possess processes capable of recording this type of data, blockchain technology has the potential to completely revolutionize the way people interact with each other.

Blockchain is a distributed data or cryptocurrency management structure with no administration, where people know nothing about each other. The whole system, given its flawless functioning, enhances the feeling of trust. Blockchain is part of the family of technologies called DLT (Distributed Ledger Technology) that were implemented to support the cryptocurrency Bitcoin, the creation of which was motivated by an extreme rejection of government-guaranteed money and bank-controlled payments. Bitcoin creator Satoshi Nakamoto's idea was for people to spend money without friction, middlemen, regulations, or the need to know or trust other parties; instead, they could simply base their trust on a functioning, transparent, and secure system.

Blockchain stores information in blocks connected together by a continuous chain (thus, it is a chain of blocks). Each time you store information in the chain you are basically adding a block without changing anything previous or rewriting anything. This is because the technology is based on a non-destructive method of recording data or changes that stores them in the ladder or ledger, keeping track of every single action and recording it chronologically. Unlike all other data storage systems, blockchain is decentralized in nature.

Decentralization allows blockchain technology to be distributed across a large network of computers spread across the world. This feature reduces the possibility of tampering with recorded data, which allows for complete trust in the data. In fact, before a block is added to the chain, a series of steps take place that make the process much more secure. Computers that receive the data and need to create a new block are tasked with solving a cryptographic puzzle and sending the solution to all other connected computers; this is the proof of work. The entire network verifies the proof of work and finally creates the block and adds it to the chain. The whole process ensures that there is full trust in every existing block.

The idea of being able to store valuable data within a secure system means that when you need that data, you don't need to pay for the services of an expert intermediary, such as a lawyer or accountant. This is because the stored data can be accessed by anyone at any time with maximum privacy. The ability to avoid intermediaries saves time and money. It is called peer-to-peer interaction, which means that it is based on an architecture in which all computers perform the function of both client and server, a system that goes against information monopolies and guarantees transparency of history and privacy. The peer-to-peer system revolutionizes the way information is recorded, verified, and transported between people. Blockchain is best defined as a technology, not a network, and can be implemented for a variety of uses. Major marketplaces of NFTs have decentralized operation and are completely based on peer-to-peer trust. This limits risk and theft. The wallets to which the stores are connected have an advanced protection system in which domains and wallet names are themselves a kind of NFT, so no one except the owner can move, withdraw, or delete the cryptocurrency contained in the wallet.

Blockchain technology is applicable to a wide range of industries, and numerous use cases continue to grow by the day. Many companies are turning to this technology for a number of benefits, including the elimination of middlemen and for faster transactions. Within the cybersecurity industry, blockchain technology has introduced new ways to store secure information and perform transactions based on trust or lack thereof (trustlessness). Digital identity is also an area that can benefit from the properties of NFTs because it is possible to store identification data with increased privacy and data integrity. A trustless system implies that the participants in the trade do not necessarily need to know each other for the system to work.

What a blockchain system allows companies to do is to examine the feasibility of transactions from the outset with no entity having authority over the system. The peer-to-peer network founded on the blockchain has transparency as its keyword. All decentralized data is made accessible and public and is verified following proof of work. Therefore, it is honest, clear, and transparent, while, simultaneously, data privacy is maintained as it is not the data itself but the strings of code associated with it that are shared. The various leaders and political and economic authorities of the world are beginning to understand the advantages of this market, appreciating the revolutionary turnaround and the incredible possibilities of use.

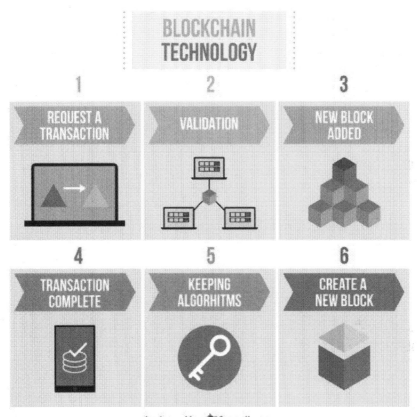

designed by freepik.com

NFT AND BLOCKCHAIN: 6 KEY PROPERTIES

Blockchain-based NFTs allow users to own digital assets. However, this ownership of digital assets is different than physical ownership because these types of assets only exist within specific, purpose-built contexts, such as marketplaces, games, and whatnot, making them more difficult to move, at least for now. When blockchain technology comes into play, it can provide a layer of coordination for digital assets, granting users' ownership and permission to manage them and changing developers' relationships with their assets. All of this is possible thanks to 6 key properties that set the rules for NFTs and represent the characteristics that make them unique.

Standardization

Standards serve to create a uniform set of rules that allow NFTs to integrate across platforms, to be interoperable, and to increase their utility value by extending their applicability.

As with all types of technologies, standards represent repeatable and shared ways of operating within a context. Standards arise from the need to save time and resources by eliminating unnecessary processes and are universally recognized within the community. A reference standard is always necessary to ensure that everyone operates in a compliant manner.

When tokenization of a digital asset takes place within blockchain, these tokens are enrolled through common, reusable, and inheritable standards. In other words, these are methods agreed upon and developed by developers that allow NFTs to operate in different ways. Each digital asset is represented differently—e.g., a game may represent its collection in an entirely different way than an event ticket. NFTs are based on a common, public system whose standards include basic features such as ownership, transfer, and access control. This means that several purchased NFTs can interoperate with each other within the same application if they are based on the same standard. Programmers can then create applications that use essentially the same code to have all tokens within a decentralized platform, such as Ethereum's network. The three main NFT tokenization standards on the Ethereum blockchain are:

- ERC721
- ERC998
- ERC1155

The acronym ERC stands for Ethereum Request for Comments. Anyone can create standards, but it is up to the author to explain them and promote support for them within the community. Since Ethereum is based on blockchain technology, there is no one person who can take over and make changes or adjustments to the protocols. ERC was created so that people could provide information or introduce new features to the Ethereum network, so ERC is how programmers propose changes to the network.

The numbers 721, 998, and 1155 represent the codes for those proposals. ERC721 was introduced in 2018 by Cryptokitties, where each cat to be adopted, nurtured, and raised was represented by a NFT. Before this standard, people could create fungible tokens such as Ether, but with ERC721, programmers can create tokens with different properties, characteristics, and types, all from the same smart contract. ERC721 is the NFT standard that allows NFTs to be created and exchanged. While it is the most popular cross-platform, easy to integrate, and available NFT standard, it also has a number of inefficiencies depending on the use case.

ERC998 has a special operation and was created to allow multiple ERC721 NFTs to be transferred within the network in a single bundle transaction instead of making several. With this standard, not only do you own an NFT, but that NFT can also include your own NFTs, as in a sort of bundle. If an NFT is sold, all the tokens attached to it are actually sold as well. Thus, transferring the composition of the NFT means transferring the entire hierarchy of associated elements. For example, a cryptokitty may own a scratching post and an eating dish that may contain fungible tokens, and in selling the cryptokitty, all of the items associated with it are also sold.

The ERC1155 token is a type of standard token that has the ability to store, within its control, tokens that can act as if they were an ERC20 or ERC721 token, or both at the same time, under the same address.

ERC1155 was created by Enjin, an Ethereum platform that allows non-fungible tokens and fungible tokens to be created in the same contract. The standardization of NFT issuance makes possible a higher degree of interoperability, which benefits users. It means that unique assets can be transferred between different applications with relative ease.

The best example of ERC1155 can be found in blockchain games. Instead of requiring a new contract for each individual game item, multiple items can be created using the same contract. Also, if, for example, both weapons and crypto coins are collectible in the game, you can write both with ERC1155, drastically reducing the resources needed to efficiently run blockchain-based games.

Interoperability

As we've already mentioned, all NFTs use the same standards just so they can be on the same level and operate on the same Ethereum platform. This enables the transfer of NFTs across multiple ecosystems, where they are immediately visible and tradable. Thus, based on the same usage characteristics—i.e. through standardization— interoperability allows NFTs to be freely tradable on open marketplaces.

Tradeability

This is the first time that users around the world can create NFTs that can be immediately available in marketplaces across the ecosystem. Here, people can buy, trade, sell, and auction NFTs. The extent of this property lies in the move from sales within closed marketplaces to the possibilities offered by a marketplace that has an open and free economy. The ease with which any user can create and then trade NFTs around the world through the blockchain is amazing.

Liquidity

This term is used to describe a level of activity within a market. The speed and efficiency of blockchain-based marketplaces leads to a high level of liquidity, which describes how many people are making trades within the marketplace and how often. High liquidity means that items are sold quickly and frequently. A marketplace based on blockchain technology allows for just such efficiency and speed in buying and exchanging, as is the case with bitcoins, which can, for example, be traded for real or fiat currency easily on Coinbase or Binance.

As with any other investment, it is necessary for anyone to be able to sell and buy tokens quickly without having to lower the price. To make this possible, the market in which you act must be liquid. In other words, there must be a high level of trading activity, and the bid and ask prices must not be too far apart.

It is very important that the NFT market has high volume and good liquidity, especially for investors who buy NFTs knowing that they have a large community of people to whom they can then sell them. For this reason, it is essential to keep an eye on the major NFT projects to invest in. To understand if a market is liquid or illiquid, the best way is to look at three indicators: trading volume in a day, the depth of the order book, and the amount that separates the bid and ask price, which is known as the bid/ask spread.

With NFTs, it is also possible to go about developing real-world asset tokenization. These NFTs could represent fractions of physical assets that can be stored and traded as tokens on a blockchain. This could introduce much-needed new liquidity into many markets that wouldn't otherwise have much, such as artwork, real estate, rare collectibles, and more.

Immutability and provable scarcity

Immutability, as the name implies, is the ability of a blockchain to remain unchanged so that it remains unaltered and indelible. To put it more simply, the data within the blockchain, as previously mentioned, cannot be changed. In its technical nature, blockchain is configured as an immutable database, and it is not possible to manipulate the data already in the blockchain.

Each block consists of information, such as the details of a transaction, and uses a cryptographic principle called a hash value. That hash value consists of an alphanumeric string generated by each block separately. Each block not only contains a hash referring to itself but also incorporates the previous one. This ensures that the blocks are paired retroactively. This is how this feature of blockchain technology ensures that no one can intrude into the system or alter the data stored in the block.

The most popular hash function is SHA256, or Secure Hash Algorithm 256. The hash value protects each block of code separately. The process of hashing generates a string of 64 characters. Regardless of the size of the input, the fixed length of the string, known as a digital signature, is always the same. This refers to the exact data entered, and the key property of this hash value is that it cannot be decoded. The word immutable is used to refer to something that can never be changed. Immutability is the key that imprints authenticity in digital assets as well as introduces scarcity. Immutability means that what belongs to a particular person in a game, for example, cannot be moved or changed.

Programmability

NFTs are fully programmable. They can, for example, be programmed to respond to triggers or actions taken by the owner. They can also respond to external triggers such as the time or score of a game. The programming possibilities of NFTs are endless.

DISCOVERING NFTS

To understand the scope of NFTs, we need to go even deeper into the recent phenomenon that has redefined the way people approach the crypto world. NFT, as already said, stands for non-fungible token. A token consists of digital information recorded in a blockchain that associates a subject with a property. These are the most well-known fungible tokens that can be used as cryptocurrencies, such as bitcoins. Bitcoins, unlike other currencies, do not have a bank behind them that distributes value. Instead, they are a system based on a network of nodes that are managed in a distributed manner. Bitcoin is just one type of cryptocurrency, none of which have a physical correspondent; instead, the money is on a public book with open access to all. Each bitcoin transaction requires considerable computing power. Bitcoins introduced the concept of trustlessness, which means that the participants involved do not need to know or trust each other as long as the system works. Real-world value is associated with such units based on the promise that a person with the asset can redeem that value for goods or services. Bitcoins strengths include immutability, non-counterfeiting, ease of transfer, robustness, and transparency.

Before the launch of blockchain technology, the cost of replicability in the digital world was almost zero. The advent of programmable digital rarity has made it possible to map the real world into the digital one. The bitcoin script language allows for a small amount of metadata to be stored on the blockchain, and these metadata are used to represent manipulation instructions. Therefore, since 2008, it has been possible to perform encoded transactions between bitcoin addresses known as "wallets." Basically, Bitcoin is a protocol that uses blockchain technology to transfer money. To provide a kind of beginner example: Just like Gmail is an application that uses the Internet to send emails, so blockchain technology can be used in many other spheres and sectors, not just in cryptocurrencies. It is often used in the financial sphere—hence, the practice of smart contracts—as it is free from hacker attacks and privacy violations. Blockchain is also an excellent solution for cloud storage, and it can provide a communication system between the machines within it.

During the process in which the transaction of any digital file in a commonly used application, such as WhatsApp, takes place, multiple copies of the same file that travel from one device to another are created. Within a distributed application in the blockchain, such as Ethereum, the file does not undergo copy creation. Instead, there is a step where a simple verification of the work takes place. Ethereum is a peer-to-peer platform based on smart contracts created in a programming language. The contracts that travel in this network do so against payment of a computational unit of account called an "ether." The ether, in addition to being a cryptocurrency, also serves as fuel for operations. This makes Ethereum suitable not only for exchanging virtual currencies but also as a network on which to run smart contracts and perform several operations such as election systems, domain name registration, crowdfunding, intellectual property, and more. During its transfer and once the token has reached the target digital account, the token remains the only copy; it just changes ownership. Blockchain technology thus allows for the preservation of the uniqueness of the transmitted digital information, and by referencing it, its value as well.

Blockchain is essentially a database with three characteristics:

> It is public. Anyone can have access to the database, and no one can own it.

➢ It is distributed in the sense that it is not located in one computer but is distributed across millions of computers around the world.
➢ It is secure. The security comes from cryptography that makes it hacker-proof.

Blockchain is a system in which digital assets are collected in encrypted form and organized via a list of all related transactions. Thus far, everyone has always considered the Internet as the medium that allows the circulation of information, but what you can't do through the Internet is transmit something of value without any intermediaries. Blockchain technology changes that by making it possible to transfer a digital asset of value from one person to another entirely digitally and without any intermediary.

Digital assets can be anything, including financial instruments, physical assets, or intangible assets such as rights. With blockchain, assets can be created. This process is called tokenization. Digital assets are based on smart contracts. These act as the system's regulators and are based on the same clauses as a typical contract; the difference is that a smart contract is totally automatic and free of intermediaries.

Crypto tokens are produced through tokenization, a process that converts the rights into an asset in the form of a cryptographically protected digital token that is tracked and traded on a blockchain network. Digital assets are often associated with the world of business and commerce. They are the resources we use to make, deliver, and capture value. Tangible assets, such as real estate, vehicles, art collections, etc., are expensive to move and transfer. Intangible assets, such as patents, copyrights, music, digital art, and trademarks, while easier to move and transfer, are difficult to partition. Fungible assets, therefore, having no specific individuality, can be substituted for one another.

When a resource is tokenized, it becomes much easier to exchange and can be made accessible from anywhere in the world. Tokens, after all, are information that can be transmitted over the Internet and tracked using a distributed ledger, the blockchain.

Cryptographic tokens usually represent a particular fungible or non-fungible resource or utility.

Fungibility refers to the interchangeability of a good; when one thing is fungible, there is also another thing that has the same value and can be exchanged for any other thing of equal value. The key difference with a non-fungible cryptographic token is that it is absolutely unique and distinct from any other; therefore, it cannot be exchanged because there is no equivalent.

An NFT is a unique ID to which specific information is attached that gives it meaning. You can link these IDs to anything physical or digital and have the ownership of the ID be the ownership of the resource, physical or digital, attributed to it. Thus, when you own an NFT, you also own all of the properties of the physical or digital resource that it represents.

Another aspect that distinguishes non-fungible tokens from fungible tokens is the standards on which their creation is based, respectively the ERC-721 or ERC-20.

The characteristics of these tokens are uniqueness, scarcity, and indivisibility, as they can only be sold, purchased, or transferred in their entirety.

Non-fungible tokens are:

- Proof of ownership of the digital resource
- A unique ID that encapsulates all of an asset's characteristics
- The rights and privileges that flow from that ownership
- Encrypted
- Registered on the blockchain

NFTs are located in the blockchain universe, and this technology allows for the intellectual property of the object in question to be proven and certified. Regardless of any transfers of ownership, its attribution will always stay in the creator's hands, while the blockchain also acts as proof of authenticity.

There are several concrete applications of NFTs that are gaining momentum. One is related to the world of art, and it can be analyzed from two points of view. First, NFTs allow tangible goods to be tokenized; thus they can represent physical works of art. Second, they have given a significant boost to the digital art market and crypto art based precisely on the exchange of digital works created by artists who have found an increasingly thriving place to buy and sell across different platforms.

SMART CONTRACTS

n this chapter, we will take a closer look at some essential concepts to better understand NFTs and how to use them:

✓ Smart contracts are protocols that facilitate and verify the negotiation and subsequent execution of the contract. These are contracts in the form of programming language.
✓ Ethereum is the decentralized platform where smart contracts are created and executed.
✓ An API (application programming interface) refers to procedures aimed at solving a given task—in this case the goal prescribed in the smart contract.
✓ The gas fee refers to a fee or value required to successfully conduct a transaction or execute a contract on a blockchain. Gas in Ethereum is a unit of measure for the work done by Ethereum to perform transactions or any interaction within the network. In Ethereum, the developers decided to attract constant values to the different operations that can be performed in Ethereum. In this way, every activity in Ethereum has a defined gas value, which does not vary and is not altered by the increase or decrease in the value of Ether, Ethereum's native currency. The fact that this gas value is constant responds to the fact that although the price of Ether is volatile, the computational cost of operations always remains constant.

Now that you know these terms, we can delve into smart contracts.

Smart contracts are computer protocols that facilitate, verify, and enforce contract negotiation. They are programs that are executed on blockchain nodes and that simulate the logic of contract clauses. The clauses and validating nodes represent a change of state of the blockchain itself; therefore, the transaction being created must find consensus through a community system. This is called "proof of work."

Within the blockchain, in fact, any type of data can be recorded and inserted in a distributed, decentralized, and transparent chain. Data validation is done through peer-to-peer verification called "proof of work" or "PoW." None of the recorded information can be deleted or modified once it is encrypted. The nodes within the blockchain, as we have seen, exchange value in an entirely new trustless situation, which involves the absence of a third figure or intermediary. Due to this nature, blockchain can hold and store all sorts of digital values and virtual assets.

The use of blockchain technology is limited to digital assets; dematerialized tangible assets can also be recorded within it. Smart contracts come into play when the data transferred on the blockchain platform must respond to predetermined conditions. Then, the platform is used to certify the transactions. Nick Szabo defined the concept of smart contracts in 1997, before blockchain. However, blockchain has played a key role in ensuring the implementation of smart contracts by allowing information and transactions to be managed securely.

A smart contract is a computer protocol that facilitates and verifies the execution of a contract between two or more users. It automatically verifies the terms based on the clauses that have been agreed upon. It is called a smart contract precisely because of its ability to be intelligent in the sense of being able to execute an agreement. It typically uses the "if/then" functions built into computer software and can only execute what has been predetermined in the programming phase. The different stages of implementing a smart contract are as follows:

• Definition of the agreement between the parties, which involves the translation and registration of the details in a smart contract.

• Related verification and inscription of the smart contract in the blockchain, where it is registered and made exclusive. The blockchain guarantees the automation of contractual obligations and their transparency in case of execution, as well as the immutability of the collected data.

The smart contract then becomes an identified block simply by transforming into a hash value that allows for the maintenance, accessibility, and correct updating of a shared ledger or distributed ledger.

The proof of work (PoW) mining inside Ethereum occurs when the miner solves the cryptographic puzzle and sends it to the whole network. At this point, the applicant of the contract pays a fee and the contract is registered.

The block is added to the immutable and certified chain. The whole operation has a public value and is completely accessible. The hashes in the sequence are safe and cannot be counterfeited.

At this point, the smart contract is able to access third-party (external) applications in order to know the conditions of certain situations and occurrences for which it was programmed—for example, to know flight times in order to communicate delays. In practice, it queries the APIs to get the necessary information. In this way, it saves a considerable number of resources in negotiation and execution, speeds up performance, and considerably decreases the chances of disputes between the parties.

Unlike a traditional contract, a smart contract is binding by its very nature—i.e., by its particular technology. The blockchain node prevents pre-established conditions from being violated, and conditions related to the conduct of the individual take a back seat. This irrevocability, which is triggered the moment the data is entered into the blockchain technology, leaves no room for exceptions.

Ethereum's virtual currency is Ether, which serves as the unit of measure and cryptocurrency. However, Ethereum, unlike Bitcoin, is not just a network for transferring value; it is a true platform for running smart contracts. Smart contracts can define rules, like a normal contract, and enforce them automatically through code. However, they are not controlled by a user. Instead, they are deployed on the network and executed as originally programmed. A smart contract on Ethereum uses the same operation as a vending machine: if you insert the coin and select the snack, you receive the snack. The vending machine follows programmed logic in the same way as a smart contract. Any programmer can write a smart contract and deploy it on Ethereum's blockchain network. Deploying a smart contract is technically a transaction, so you will have to have Ether to pay the gas fee just like a normal transaction. However, the costs of implementing the contract are much higher.

Since each Ethereum transaction requires computing resources to be executed, each transaction requires a fee. Gas is the fee required to successfully conduct a transaction on Ethereum. Both the ether and gas gee on Ethereum are essential to keep the network secure in order to prevent any spam.

Ethereum has developer-friendly languages for writing smart contracts, such as Solidity and Vyper. Smart contracts are public on Ethereum and can be thought of as open APIs. This allows smart contracts to be composable. Moreover, you can start a smart contract on an existing one. It is also possible to enable a self-destruct option, which aims to remove programs that are no longer used to improve effectiveness and performance.

With the help of smart contracts, digital assets can be programmed in such a way as to have additional functions compared to traditional modes. Digital assets based on a smart contract can execute clauses completely autonomously, without the intermediation of third parties, thus increasing transparency and legal security. For this reason, they have many possibilities within different areas and applications, such as the following:

• **Cybersecurity:** Although it is a system visible to everyone, everything in the blockchain is inscribed through encrypted keys that allow the verification of the data within it, and the transmission of data is protected from interception and manipulation.

• **Election systems:** Blockchain enables voter identity authentication, secure record keeping, and accurate and transparent counting.

• **Internet of Things (IoT):** When objects become smart and talk to each other they can facilitate and verify the execution of operations within an enterprise. Smart contracts provide the backbone for the Internet of Things and allow for a ledger that can manage a large number of devices.

• **Public administration:** Can offer monitoring to ensure secure and transparent governance.

• **Crowdfunding**: Enables campaigns where contributors can have full control of the money invested. In this way, the donor is more secure and the money is not spent on intermediary activities.

• **Intellectual property**: The very structure of blockchain allows you to keep track of everything, including transactions and change of ownership. This is why smart contracts find application in tracking individual properties with chronological accuracy.

Smart contracts

1. Smart Contract Explained

✓ A contract is created between two parties

✓ Both parties remain anonymous

✓ The contract is stored on a public ledger

✓ some triggering events are set i.e. deadlines

✓ The contract self-executes as per written codes

✓ Regulators and users can analyze all the activities.

✓ Predict market uncertainties and trends

2. How Do Smart Contracts Work

✓ Matchmaking of Seller and Buyer
✓ TRANSACTION
✓ Recieving assets Assets Distribution

Registered

Automated Settlement of Contracts

No third party need

3. Smart Contracts Benefits

Secured

Autonomous

Accurate, Always

Interruption Free

Fast Performance

Trustless

Cost Effective

4. Smart Contracts Use Cases

Record Storing

Trading Activities

Supply Chains

Mortgage

Real Estate Market

Employment Arrangement

Copyright Protection

Healthcare services

Government Voting

Insurance Claims

Internet-of-things (IoT)

CRYPTO DUKEDOM

DIGITAL ASSETS

Now it's time to explore the world of digital assets. A digital asset can be any digital document, sound content, image, etc. that is transported in a digital format. A digital asset is a digitally stored piece of content. More precisely, it is a self-contained collection of binary data that is uniquely identifiable and has some value. This is because binary data is easily understood by a computer. The three main characteristics of a digital asset are:

- The digital nature
- Unique identification
- Value

Any digital asset has a value, but not all values are established in the same way. It's a pretty diverse world since virtually anything can become a digital asset, but through smart contracts and blockchain technology, digital assets can be programmed to be issued or traded as assets.

Digital assets carried on blockchain also inscribe within them all their token's transactions and movements. The digital asset standard introduced by Ethereum in 2015 is ERC20, and it is the most widely used. Digital assets can be smart-contracted and programmed to perform various functions autonomously and without an intermediary. Once the digital token has been issued on the blockchain, it is transmitted to the network and distributed following the payment of a fee. At this point, the digital assets can be traded within a community of investors.

In practice, the moment the protocol has been established or the smart contract "deployed" on blockchain, the digital assets are mined or transferred to the public address of the issuer. Each public address is assigned a private key that allows the owner of the tokens to sign the transaction related to the transfer of digital assets from his address to another. The custody of digital assets refers to the possession of a private key that is linked to the public address where the digital assets are kept.

The domain and ownership of an NFT is verifiable by anyone. NFT creators can sell their work, which corresponds to a unique ID worldwide in the Ethereum network. They can claim the copyright on the token and those of resale of the same.

Each NFT features the following:

- A unique ID.
- It is not interchangeable with other tokens.
- Ownership information on the token is always verifiable.
- It is based on Ethereum and can be sold or purchased on any Ethereum-based NFT marketplace.
- It cannot be manipulated.
- It can be resold if resale rights have been earned.
- It cannot be deleted from the Ethereum wallet.

The creator of an NFT can prove ownership, earn royalties every time it is sold, or sell it independently on any NFT marketplace platform without involving any third party. It is the creator of the NFT who decides the scarcity of their digital asset. Often creators generate multiple editions of their tokens, each of which is unique.

NFT – AREAS AND USES

For a digital content creator, an NFT is important because it allows them to maximize earnings that will not be sucked up by any platforms and/or intermediaries for sales, commissions, and fees of various kinds. Platforms often earn more than creators when they display an artist's work because of the possibility of exposure. In the case of NFTs, however, creators do not transfer ownership of the digital content to the platform. Instead, ownership is intrinsic to the token itself, embedded in the content. The funds raised from the sale of the content belong to the creator, who can also claim royalties. Owning a digital asset is valuable because the marketplace makes it so through verifiable ownership.

NFTs have seen a lot of interest from online game developers because they can provide deeds of ownership for in-game items and bring a number of benefits to players. In many of the world's most popular games, it is already possible to purchase in-game items that can be used to, for example, customize and/or equip your characters or achieve winnings. If that object was an NFT, it would be possible to recover the money spent reselling it once the game is finished. If the purchased accessory increases interest and value, then you can easily generate some profit as well.

One of the possible uses of NFTs that is growing more and more is that of decentralized finance. Thanks to the use of smart contracts, the transaction takes place with total security. There are decentralized platforms or DeFi that allow you to borrow money against collateral. The automatic clauses of smart contracts ensure that the creditor is reimbursed. On the other hand, the NFT itself can be a guarantee to access a loan. If the creditor is not repaid, the crypto object is sent directly to the creditor's wallet.

As a recent and rapidly expanding technology, the world of NFTs has yet to be fully explored, and new possible uses pop up every day. There are many of them, and they all represent potential profitable areas of investment, gain, and implementation that could also innovate many "non-digital" sectors

MAIN USES

The overwhelming reach of NFTs is gaining ground in more and more areas and sectors, from the corporate sector, where it solves problems of smart recognition, to the gaming world, where fans from all over the world enjoy increased possibilities of personalization.

Other possible uses of NFTs are in the fashion industry and in the big brands, where real products can be placed side-by-side with digital assets that have been intentionally created to be unique and original. Moreover, not even the real estate market is immune to NFTs: today, a virtual plot of land can be worth as much as a real one in the center of New York. However, it is the uniqueness of NFTs that breaks through to the sentimental value of investors and collectors around the world.

INTELLIGENT IDENTITY

Blockchain technology and NFTs are playing an increasingly important role in the digital economy. Their ability to represent digital objects that are unique to the world is widely exploitable due to the principle that a unique object is more valuable. The attributes that NFTs can incorporate can be pretty complex, and each NFT can have increasingly dynamic and smart information, as we have seen concerning smart contract automations. Many companies will be able to take advantage of these features by applying NFTs to software licenses. For instance, a key, a unique and complex string, can be required to access company software. NFTs in your wallet, browser, or mobile device will speed up access and identity verification. NFTs are perfect for breaking down attempts at identity fraud.

All documents can be digitized to represent identities such as qualifications, references, and physical appearance; this application of NFTs requires the transformation or digitization of documents into unique tokens that can be used for identity recognition. NFTs could make some exciting systemic changes in this area.

GAMING

In addition to the corporate sector, many industries are discovering the benefits of NFTs, chief among them the gaming world. Gamers use NFTs to exchange digital assets and earn more points playing video games. Tokens have the advantage of being authenticated and verifiable by all participants in a game. NFTs allow gamers to fully utilize their gaming skills and generate real-time revenue, such as buying and selling weapons, vehicles, and characters. Within the gaming industry, it might be safe to say that NFTs are already more than just a trend.

For instance, with NBA Top Shot created by Dapper Labs, the NBA is already investing in NFTs. What is happening in gaming is that many people claim ownership of digital items and are willing to spend a lot to own extremely rare and hard-to-get gaming items. NFTs allow players to celebrate their accomplishment in obtaining a very rare gaming item, which could be literally anything. Also, because they are non-fungible tokens, these items gain added value because of their rarity, uniqueness, and right to be claimed. Weapons, items, character skins, etc. increase the rarity, cost, and importance of the game. Besides, these properties can be sold and gain even more value.

Today, with NFTs, you can take properties with you, sell them, collect them, and move on to another game. The benefit is primarily emotional/affective: it is gratifying to know that you can own a clip of the NBA team—not as a mere collectible, but as a keepsake that achieves emotional value before monetary value. Moreover, the value of the assets is part of the gaming experience.

FASHION

NFTs offer new ways for consumers to collect, wear, and trade fashion items online. Now that most fashion shows have been scaled back or gone virtual, they could become an essential tool for the fashion industry. A new chapter is about to open for the digital art story: brands are pushing the emotional, nostalgic, and sentimental sides of the NFT factor.

There is a big advantage for brands that start creating fashion-related NFTs. For example, Argentinean designer Andrés Reisinger sold ten virtual pieces of furniture in an online auction, with the most expensive item reaching almost $70,000. Virtual furniture, auctioned through Nifty Gateway, can be used within rooms such as Decentraland or Somnium Space. Targeting this growing market has a positive effect on the brand's visibility online and, therefore, brings in new viewers. "Iconic pieces," "limited editions," and "luxury" are keywords that have always been part of the fashion industry.

Today, projects like The Dematerialized represent the vanguard of digital fashion. Arguably in the near future, fashion will not be able to do without NFTs. The development of limited edition virtual goods such as clothes, shoes, and fashion accessories with which an NFT is associated proves the ownership of that good and the realization in limited and special edition. In a mixed perspective, halfway between digital and material, a person can buy a real product belonging to the fashion industry and, at the same time, receive an NFT and a digital version of the same product to use in online games, which extends the value of the object in both spaces.

The scarcity of the good and the limited supply amplifies the sense of exclusivity traditionally associated with luxury goods and represents an advantage in terms of brand visibility. NFTs use in the fashion industry responds to the needs and demands of the public. Many people want to show off their unique products in a virtual gallery or wallet or by having them worn by game characters or avatars, so there is a market with a high level of liquidity.

CRYPTO ART

A younger generation is approaching the art world by opening an alternative, less intimidating, and more transparent market. Collecting is no longer the preserve of an exclusive and privileged class. Cryptographic art in blockchain allows those who wish to do so to support an artist's work. Artists gain the advantages of visibility and more transparent earnings through smart contracts and royalties. Plus, work in crypto art allows one to experiment, hone skills, and tell a story from one's point of view. The best artists, those who also know how to tell a story and showcase their personalities, eliminate the middlemen and establish a close relationship with fans.

The distinguishing factors for cryptographic digital art are the possibility granted to artists to maintain their rights to their works and the ability for novice artists to think and move within the crypto art world on par with traditional and established artists. Digital art has always been reproducible, and within the digital artwork industry, there were a lot of ownership and rights issues. With crypto art, works can be seen by sharing their images on social media or the web, but only the person who buys them has ownership; thus, the artist also protects their rights.

MUSIC

The person who can best explain the possible applications of NFT in the music industry is Mike Shinoda, co-founder of Linkin Park. Although verifiable digital scarcity has become all the rage, he was ready to embrace this new business model even before the public heard about it. Today, his single "Happy Endings" was sold in NFT for about $10,000, with all proceeds going to the ArtCenter College of Design in Pasadena, California.

Emulating what Mike Shinoda has done, many other artists are coming up with music projects that can depopulate the crypto art market—in this case, music, which carries with it many copyright issues and discussions.

The music ecosystem thought it could take advantage of the Internet to help create a community around music and allow musicians to take control of their music and make a living without having to be part of the music industry. But even with Napster, iTunes, Spotify, and others—all services that were meant to bring music closer to fans—that wasn't the case. The distribution system continued to reap profits on the backs of many musicians. To this day, most artists receive about 12% of all profits generated by their art. Basically, the streaming platforms have become the middlemen.

The gap between the value that music brings to people's lives and the price they pay for it is huge, and a song that can change people's lives is worth far more than the few cents the artists gets from a stream. NFTs provide a new business model that allows artists to value their music appropriately, reconnect with audiences, and challenge the old order of things.

COLLECTIBLES

The most basic application of non-fungible tokens comes in the form of digital collectibles and in-game purchases. These are items that artists have developed themselves or licensed from pre-existing brands. For example, DC Comics recently began exploring the world of NFTs, and from now on, artists cannot sell tokens representing their intellectual property.

Both artists and collectors of crypto works assess the value of their products according to the following measures: intrinsic value (i.e., if they like the object on a personal level), extrinsic value (i.e., if owning that token makes them look cooler), by utility (if, for example, it can be used in a game), or as an investment (if that particular NFT can maintain or increase its value). For investors and collectors, the primary purpose of NFTs is for them to increase in value. The best collectors value discretion and exclusivity. Rarity is a distinguishing factor; this is what the Rare Pepe Foundation and the famous meme are based on. Many have started buying and selling limited edition cryptographic Pepe collectible cards developed by artists and issued by the Rare Pepe Foundation. Buyers subsequently store these in Rare Pepe wallets.

Non-fungible tokens can even present an opportunity for endangered species conservation and environmental tourism. Collectibles are sometimes referred to as "emotional assets" or "passion investments." NFTs could be used as an alternative means of wildlife conservation and funding for environmental groups. Collectible animals could carry with them all the characteristics of the endangered species in the form of metadata. This could be extended to virtual environments as well.

REAL ESTATE

The digital real estate sector provides for a cost of production of land that borders on zero. Its true value is precisely linked to its uniqueness, to the fact of owning an asset—or, rather, an original and unique token. Here, the convergence between the real and the digital reaches its highest expression. It becomes a thin line of demarcation that is almost impossible to see. In places like Decentraland, it is possible to have your own store with digital assets linked to a clothing chain and much more. Several artists have created NFT villas and collections to visit as well as huge virtual events. On these marketplaces, the value of a property or piece of land becomes much higher than the real thing, and a digital property is sold in a second without any need for a middleman.

To better clarify the opportunities that the real estate sector could exploit with NFTs, it is enough to take the example of the Canadian architect Krista Kim who sold her digital house for 288 ether, the equivalent of $512,000. In this way, the architect brought her meditative design concept into the realm of digital assets. The purchase of this designer home allows the owner to place it within a metaverse, a term that describes a collaborative virtual world in which to experience real estate.

A virtual land or property offers the same investment possibilities as the sale of real estate: it is possible to invest in land, build hotels, or put up stores, although the minimum investment is around $25,000. The digital real estate world is growing rapidly, and so are the dedicated projects. We will follow up with NFT developments in this area by providing a dedicated guide soon.

HOW TO CREATE, BUY AND SELL A NON-FUNGIBLE TOKEN

Managing NFTs is much easier than it sounds, especially after understanding their facets and properties, the underlying blockchain technology, and the essential function of a smart contract. Non-fungible tokens can virtually represent an endless array of objects, such as artworks, motion designs, GIFs, virtual objects within video games (such as skins, weapons, and avatars), and much more, following the futuristic and artistic visions of those who create them.

As we have seen, however, it doesn't end there. It is also possible to transform music into NFT, as well as collectible cards, cars, houses, animals, designer sneakers, virtual terrains, and clips of iconic sports videos. For example, the creation of a graphic image, a .jpg, to be placed on the Ethereum blockchain, is now the leading NFT blockchain service.

But there are others, such as EOS, Flow from Dapper Labs, and many more. The difference in choosing a service lies in the fact that each of them is based on a different standard, and it is necessary to take this into account based on the purpose for which you want to create the NFT and where you then want to use it because the standards can change from wallet to wallet. To turn the image into NFT art, you will need:

• An Ethereum wallet or a wallet that supports the ERC721 standard, including MetaMask, Trust Wallet, or Coinbase Wallet.

• To turn $50 or $100 into ether or ETH, the currency on which Ethereum is based. There are many accepted currencies, from the dollar to the pound to the euro, or you can buy ether directly from another cryptocurrency.

MetaMask is a cryptocurrency wallet that allows you to interact with decentralized platforms based on Ethereum directly in your browser. It is compatible with Chrome, Firefox, and Opera and enables you to exchange cryptocurrency in ether form and manage ERC20 tokens and non-fungible tokens in ERC721. Moreover, it is a highly secure wallet and offers advanced dApp integration with the ability to make purchases through dematerialized apps.

INSTALLING METAMASK

Step 1. Go to: https://metamask.io/

Step 2. Click "Get Chrome Extension" to install Metamask.

Step 3. Click "Add to Chrome" in the upper right.

Step 4. Click "Add Extension" to complete the installation.

Once downloaded, activating and using it is a breeze. To be so secure, MetaMask uses keys so that you can recover your money. Once it is installed, you'll find it in your browser bar represented by a small logo in the shape of a fox.

Once you log in with your chosen password, 12 words will appear in sequence for you to memorize and enter on the next screen. At this point, MetaMask will have created an Ethereum address.

CREATE A WALLET

To do this, follow the instructions below.

Step 1. Click on the Metamask logo in the upper right-hand corner of your Google chrome browser.

Step 2. Read and agree to the terms and conditions. You may have to agree to 2 to 3 pages worth of terms.

Step 3. Enter a password and click "*Create*" to create your wallet.

Step 4. You will see a set of 12 "seed words" for your vault. Click "*Save Seed Words as File*" and copy the "*Metamask Seed Words*" file that is downloaded to a safe place. You will need it to access your vault.

Step 5. Click "*I've Copied It Somewhere Safe*" once your seed words file has been secured. You'll be taken into your Metamask wallet.

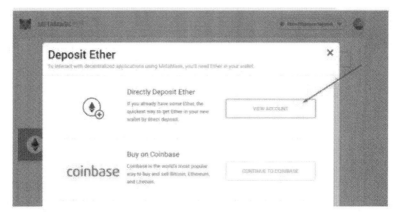

DEPOSITING FUNDS
➢ Click on **View Account**.
➢ You can now see your **public address** and share it with other people. MetaMask offers **different methods to buy** coins, but you can do it differently as well.
   You just need your address.
The MetaMask extension will regularly be available in your browser's toolbar.
It's easily accessible, and as you saw from these steps, simple to use as well. Sending coins is also very intuitive; there is a big send button, and the rest are easily understandable.

Sites such as Coinbase are ideal for exchanging currencies such as dollars for cryptocurrencies. By creating an account on Coinbase, you can access a wallet into which you can transfer money from your bank or PayPal account. Using ETH in the Coinbase wallet, you can transfer money to your MetaMask crypto wallet connected to the marketplace. Now, you are ready to coin your first NFT.

Major marketplaces such as OpenSea, Rarible, and Mintable have a "create" function. For example, on one of the biggest marketplaces, OpenSea, you just click on the button in the upper right corner to create NFTs and connect your wallet through the password. Then, you can create your personal folder and enrich it with a profile picture and cover photo. When making your own NFTs, you can add all the properties and unique attributes that increase the NFTs' scarcity and value.

The creator also has the opportunity to add content that only the buyer can access. Marketplaces let you upload many file formats, either static images or animation. To put your non-fungible digital objects up for sale, all you have to do is write a description of the work, add tags that will allow the NFT to be found, and set the price through the "buy it now" option or set a minimum bid if you want collectors to bid on the auctioned piece.

Also, you can put up a single copy or multiple editions of the same work for sale, but the more editions that are created, the less valuable the piece will be perceived to be. Once all the options are set, you will make the file's actual drop, which is when it is effectively tokenized and inserted into your wallet. Entering the token pricing options gives you the ability to schedule royalties that allow NFT creators to earn a commission every time the resource is sold to a new person.

All of this can create passive income streams that last for the life of the artist and are automatically triggered by smart contracts. A price may be charged to place a work on a marketplace, and it can vary depending on the store chosen. The tokenization or minting process has an associated fee called a gas fee that must be paid with Ethereum. Gas fees are essentially the cost of electricity for all the computers that calculate the transaction and tokenize the work. These gas fees can differ and change at any time based on the demand of calculation.

To start making huge gains with crypto art, being an established digital artist on social media or being a celebrity helps a lot. This is a vast sea to swim in, and having an online presence can help build interest in your work. The art that you can make doesn't have to have all the same aesthetics; originality could be a distinguishing factor. For a young artist creating your first non-fungible tokens, it's crucial to be true to yourself, to make things that you are passionate about, and to be able to convey your passion to others.

HOW TO BUY A NON-FUNGIBLE TOKEN

NFTs have made the rounds on the web because of the great sales made by artists like Beeple, singers like Grimes, entrepreneurs like Jack Dorsey, and many others who are discovering this world every day. Behind these sales is more than just the hype or gamble that many people associate with the world of NFTs. In reality, these are investments that can be calculated and reasoned and that are based on several prerogatives that make the purchase consistent and valuable:

1. **The notoriety of the NFT creator**. Simply put, the creator, brand, or genre that creates the NFT should be famous, which involves a more considerable investment, but usually renowned people or big brands have a good following.
2. **First Edition**. It matters a lot to secure the first edition of the NFT in question because people always want a piece of history, and it will be possible to profit from the resale of the asset.
3. **A tangible NFT** is a good investment because it allows you to have both a digital property and a tangible asset. Anything that can be associated with the non-tangible asset is added value.

4. **Scarcity** is imperative because the rarer an item is, the more valuable it is.

Being an NFT buyer involves having a certain kind of market focus and a good dose of smarts. Art doesn't look at rankings, but collectors often use OpenSea's rankings page to discover new and exciting creators. It's a matter of initially understanding what kind of NFT you intend to buy and what kind of standards it is based on. This is because some of them are only present on specific platforms, and you need to have an account on the platform you're using and be able to connect your wallet to it. For example, to buy NBA Top Shot, you need to open an account with and create a wallet on Drapper, and you need to have stablecoin USDC currency. It is also important to understand the distribution of NFT projects. Some communities isolate themselves around a single project, such as Gods Unchained players, but some enthusiasts play with CryptoKitties and actively participate in the interchange between communities.

What is certain is that entering the world of NFTs at this time is an advantage. It is a trend that is not destined to disappear and in which investments are profitable. Virtual worlds are expanding. New native blockchain worlds are being born that are more and more cutting edge and simplified. Their development is increasingly driven by market demands. Cryptovoxels is a good example. It has a similar operation to Decentraland in which the most exciting element is the ability to show NFTs purchased within the world. In contrast, the virtual world projects are, like Somnium Space or High Fidelity from the creators of Second Life, allow you to virtually showcase of your NFTs.

WHAT ARE NFTS?

Non-fungible tokens are a special-grade digital asset where every single token or item is unique. Because of these characteristics, NFTs can't be interchanged or replaced with identical tokens.

BUY

SELL

HOW TO BUY NFT?

01 Choose an NFT marketplace that lets users buy and sell non-fungible tokens

02 Create an account in your chosen NFT marketplace

03 Sign up for a blockchain wallet and connect that wallet to your NFT account

04 Buy Ether or other supported digital currency from a crypto exchange and fund your blockchain wallet

05 Browse through the marketplace listings and choose the NFT you want to buy

 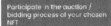

06 Participate in the auction / bidding process of your chosen NFT

07 Based on the bidding amount, you may or may not own the NFT (The NFT is awarded to the highest bidder)

HOW TO CREATE AND SELL NFTS

Choose a marketplace that lets users create NFTs and create an account

Connect your blockchain wallet to the account and fund it

Select the contents that you want to turn into NFTs and upload them to your account

Pay the minimum fee for creating the NFT (The fee varies from marketplace to marketplace)

Once uploaded, select the NFT you want to sell and set a fixed price or a bidding range

Promote your NFT on social media to gain prospective buyers

Once a buyer buys your NFT (generally through bidding), the payment automatically gets stored in your blockchain wallet

10 DISRUPTIVE PROJECTS

Beeple's artwork displayed on a smartphone. Dollars background.

Here is our selection of the 10 most interesting NFT projects so far.

1. **Mike Winkelmann**, aka **Beeple**, sold his NFT titled "The First 5,000 Days" and challenged the whole world to consider how disruptive NFTs can be. The piece depicts a collage of all the digital works Beeple had created since 2007.
2. **Nyan Cat**, the animated GIF featuring a cat flying through space followed by a rainbow and created by Chris Torres, sold for nearly $580,000.

3. Grimes sold **WarNymph Collection** Vol. 1 for the equivalent of $5.8 million, while many other musicians have made record figures and revolutionized the industry. Kings of Leon, for example, generated sales of about $1.45 million by tokenizing their album and jumping into the NFT market.
4. **Cryptopunks** is the project that inspired the whole crypto art movement. It features 10,000 unique characters to collect with proof of ownership stored on the Ethereum blockchain. Cryptopunks are 24x24-pixel algorithmically generated art images. Most are punk-looking boys and girls, but there are some monkeys, zombies, and even aliens.
5. **Authoglyphs** is a generative art experiment project from LarvaLabs. Each Authoglyphs is unique and created by executing code on the Ethereum blockchain. The idea behind these glyphs is that each one can be made by anyone who is willing to donate the creation fee of 0.20 Eth (about 525$) to the 350.org charity. The maker of the glyph will then also become the first owner of the glyph.
6. The best example of projects aimed at charities and NFTs is **Cryptokitties' Honu**. Ocean Elders and ACTAI Global partnered to create an exclusive CryptoKitty that was auctioned off to generate funds to save the oceans.
7. The **PandaEarth** Collection, available on OpenSea, is a game centered around delightful reproducible, collectible, and adorable creatures in the form of digital pandas living in the blockchain. Each panda comes from the true descendants of 50 giant pandas officially licensed by China's Panda Conservation and Research Center to be reproduced on the blockchain.
8. **World of Ether** is a duel-based game where you collect monsters, which must be bred and trained for combat, in a decentralized way. Each monster is based on a smart contract and referenced by the platform.
9. **CryptoZombies** is an interactive school that teaches all of the blockchain techniques and how to make smart contracts in Solidity. With CryptoZombies, you can learn how to create

your own collectible game. Inside, there are step-by-step lessons to develop a blockchain-based game.

10. **Codex Protocol** deals with digital assets of real objects. On the platform, you can verify the authenticity of a collectible and view its provenance, identity, and history. The art and collectibles market often contains counterfeit or defective pieces because they rely on an antiquated validation system. Codex Protocol is a solution to this problem because it is a new structure that is simple, secure, and immutable.

NFTS - PROS, CONS AND THE FUTURE

Depending on the industry and application, NFTs have several demonstrable and revolutionary benefits. Within art, there are many existing digital works whose provenance could not be protected prior to this technology. By introducing the principle of scarcity and uniqueness, NFTs have redistributed power within a world monopolized by galleries, auction houses, and investors.

Art projects such as Beeple's do not generate such hype simply because of the cost of individual works, but rather because of the change and revolutionary impact they represent in the art market and beyond. The fact that works of art required large sums of money to own was already a fact, a custom; they are unique objects that wealthy buyers from all over the world make their own.

Today, tokenized art is visible to anyone, some works are within everyone's reach, and everyone can access a marketplace and enter a contemporary art gallery with the possibility of becoming the owner of a unique and valuable piece. Thus, artists can also showcase themselves according to their own preferences. The democratization of art starts here.

What many people continue to wonder is why they should pay to have something that would be easy to download and store on their computer. The problem is that the downloaded image on your computer has no real value; it can't have the same value as the original image. It's exactly like downloading an image of a Picasso: no matter how good the resolution is on an image that represents an unquestionably valuable subject, it will never have the same value as the original.

The value of cryptographic art is based on scarcity and non-reproducibility. What is difficult to understand is that the true public value of the purchase made is not only the work and what it represents, which is reserved for the personal sphere, but actually resides in the token itself.

For other applications, however, the value is based on the ability of NFTs to be transferable. This allows, for example, game enthusiasts to be able to buy several NFTs and collect them within another platform. This ability, due to the creation of peer-to-peer standards, makes NFTs even more desirable.

Within the gaming world, spending money in order to have a certain skin for in-game characters was customary even before the appearance of NFTs. Minting an NFT means making that skin authentic and traceable back to its original owner at all times. Thus, it is the blockchain technology that makes it feasible for NFTs to take on value, and it is the same technology that makes possible their applications in business, industry, gaming, art, music, tourism, real estate, and much more in the future.

However, even the most revolutionary of technologies holds faces challenges, problems, and potential drawbacks. For instance, many creatives, finally protected and recognized in their rights, may look for easy money and start to increase the editions of their works in an excessive way. Making too many editions of the same work would lead to an inevitable devaluation of the NFT and a consequent impoverishment of the very idea of uniqueness that NFTs represent.

The digital art market is bigger than most think. That's why some platforms have provided selection criteria by which creators can sell their art, making access challenging. Furthermore, as much as this world of crypto art may be within the reach of potentially many more people, it is often reserved for experienced investors who have already profited from this sector and for whom owning digital assets is a cultural marker. This should not be discouraged. That this market will become mainstream for many is only a matter of time. Change is in the air, and the potential is endless.

Marketplaces are a good showcase for artists, but determining how to be seen and talked about is often up to the creator, who is responsible for engaging with their audience through specific channels, such as Reddit, Twitter, or Telegram. Today, crypto art represents the best alternative option to traditional art for emerging artists. However, there is a hyperactivity between supply and demand, meaning continuous movement that results in hyper production and hyper consumption, which makes it difficult for some artists to emerge and be seen.

A great debate has arisen around the ecological issue of NFTs, which involves the environmental impact of the crypto world. This infrastructure is powered by electricity, which is mainly produced by fossil fuels that account for 64% of the world's electricity (coal 38%, oil and gas 26%).

The use of fossil fuels involves the emission of CO_2, which can be naturally reabsorbed by trees, but if this exceeds the capacity of absorption, carbon dioxide accumulates in the atmosphere, causing pollution, temperature rise, sea level rise, total loss of entire species, and countless severe weather events.

The words of Seth Godin, famous marketing guru and creator of Tribe, seem to sum up the problem: "And so creators and buyers are then hooked into a cycle, with all of us paying the duration of the costs associated with an unregulated system that consumes huge amounts of precious energy for no other purpose than to create a few scarce digital tokens," defining the whole system of NFTs as a trap into which many have stumbled.

A single Ether consumes about the equivalent amount of electricity as an EU resident in 4 days. In addition, NFTs involve more complex transactions and multiple chain reactions, such as bids, sells, and property exchanges. Still, the possibilities that crypto art and NFTs are offering to young artists and others are considerable. This is why so much frenzy and excitement has been created around it.

The solution cannot be to stop everything and trash such a technology; it must be to find effective solutions to lower the ecological footprint of the creation and marketing of NFTs. It is essential to make the world population more and more aware of environmental issues and to think together about valid solutions to the problems that arise.

For example, artist Memo Akten launched an extraordinary investigation and created a set of tools to evaluate everyone's crypto wallet. Evaluating solutions that include greater transparency from major marketplaces, focusing on renewable energy resources, or minimizing on-chain transactions could be far more useful for the future of the crypto world and the real world than pointing fingers and blaming consumers or emerging artists. The ecological impact of proof of work (PoW) was already known from the beginning, but not giving up on this technology is essential to be able to innovate the world. The decisive step for us is raising people's awareness and activating a proactive process aimed at concrete problem-solving rather than sterile accusations and judgments.

What has to change is the mentality, the awareness, and the desire to create a sustainable world. We should realize by now that progress is unstoppable and always involves advantages and disadvantages. We are here today to increase the former and decrease the latter for the common good of all.

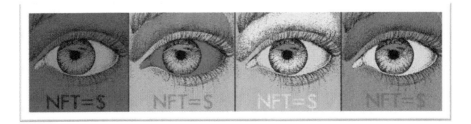

CRYPTO ART
REVOLUTION

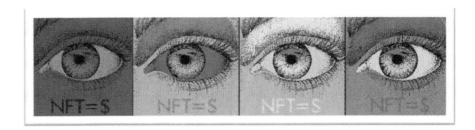

This guide is aimed at digital artists, designers, and all those who have become curious about the world of crypto art and NFTs. However, if what got you here is not just curiosity but a genuine desire to become part of the world of crypto art, either as a creator or an investor, it's time to start investigating all the facets of the phenomenon without just getting carried away by the hype, but by actively participating in the change. We are here to help you better understand how to position yourself within the crypto art market and prepare for an incredible new expansion of the art world.

CRYPTO ART VS. TRADITIONAL ART MARKET

C rypto art is a very new artistic movement through which the artist produces artwork in the form of still or motion pictures, which are then animated in collaboration with the computer, and distributed using blockchain technology.

The blockchain is a distributed system that enables anyone to upload data, images, videos, and any other type of digital resource to a secure and stable virtual register that allows to identify ownership, track movements, and give a unique value to one's work. Crypto art is a movement that subverts traditional art because the blockchain network does not present any barrier, neither for artists nor the consumers.

The change brought about by this new technology is making the rounds of the web, and it's all anyone is talking about. Curiosity regarding the phenomenon and what changes it could bring to the art world as we know it has increased. Basically, when the work of art, for instance, the image in digital .jpg format, is transformed into a token, it becomes part of the artist's cryptographic portfolio. And when a creator adds a digital asset to a digital gallery, a token is generated and deposited in the artist's wallet through a smart contract that acts as a regulator of the system and is based on the same clauses as an ordinary agreement. Still, a smart contract is entirely automatic and does not require intermediaries.

The token is indelibly linked to the artwork and is a unique asset that represents the ownership and authenticity of the underlying artwork. Once offered for sale on Ethereum's blockchain network, the art piece takes on a unique code, solely attributable to it, thus distinguishing its content. This way, this single image can be distributed in multiple nodes of the network and can always be sold while keeping unchanged code and metadata, like, for example, the properties that describe the work itself and can be identified conceptually as the only digital resource or asset available. It is confirmed at this point that anyone can see the work, which can be reproduced countless times. However, its copies are not very valuable. The token associated with the art piece, on the other hand, is the real work of art; it is unique. Like physical galleries or museums, blockchain-based platforms allow anyone to come in, admire the artwork, and browse through it. But even though the work remains visible to all and is reproducible, only the collector who buys it can claim ownership of what the artist has called the original, the unique token of the work. Of course, the buyer must understand that they own digital artwork and not a physical object to hang on the wall. And here, many prejudices belonging to a generation that evaluates the value of the object for its material weight rather than its intrinsic value — a concept that millennials and subsequent generations often better understand — must be debunked.

In traditional art, several factors make a specific piece of art valuable, such as its provenance, condition, authenticity, display, and quality. By linking digital art to non-fungible tokens, it is possible to trace similar characteristics, such as authenticity, to traditional art in crypto art. Yet, as with economic currency, the commercial value of the artwork is based on collective intentionality. Indeed, value is not objective nor extrinsic; the human stipulation or statement is what comes to give commercial value to the artwork.

What many tend not to consider is that the way things are done today has changed. It's true of gaming, finance, real estate, and collecting, but there is still a bias against digital art. The problem that arose for digital art was its reproducibility, the loss of its aura due to the possibility of copying it, as postulated by Walter Benjamin. However, crypto art has definitely brought uniqueness to the digital world. Although some artists question its ability to compete with the traditional market, the crypto art market is growing fast. Damien Hirst has even announced that he is riding crypto art by putting up for sale as many as 10,000 original works created long ago on paper and currently locked away in a vault. Hirst said his creations are about to come to life through the launch on the blockchain, at which time they will exist as NFTs.

Digital art exists since the advent of computers, and digital art's significant challenge - rarity - has been overcome through the emergence of NFTs. NFTs work on a decentralized basis, eliminating the middlemen in the physical world for traditional art. Some platforms allow artists to manage their work and get royalties and commissions on primary and secondary sales, all based on a trust system built by the network itself, where the parties do not need to know each other to proceed with the transaction.

However, the aspect that remains tied to the traditional art market is the artwork's valuation, which is appropriately subjective. Artists who are already famous surely have a way to raise the prices of their works and are more likely to see their art pieces get bought due to the possibility for the buyer to make a future profit or for simply collecting it. But it's a substantially different market, more democratic and open to young emerging artists who have been experimenting with the digital environment for a long time. Digital art has never replaced traditional art, and NFTs probably won't either because conventional art is historically influential enough to be supplanted. Its value persists to this day. Indeed, one might say it has gained even more, not in the sense of money, but rather in the sense of possibility, openness, newness, and freshness.

Cryptographic art is one of the few artistic movements of this millennium that speaks the language of its time, a new digital expression tailored to the new generation of collectors and creators. If until recently, an artist who created digital artworks had very few chances to put them on the market due to their infinite reproducibility, today, thanks to the blockchain, these digital artworks are made in limited edition, and therefore, acquire an exchange value.

Unlike in the traditional art world, crypto artists do not ask permission from gallery owners, agents, auction houses, or others to share and sell their works. They simply leverage the blockchain and decide on their own to showcase their work and make it available to the public.

CRYPTO ART: AN OVERVIEW

To be concise, crypto art is an art movement that uses blockchain technology for its creation and distribution. Blockchain technology is a system that works in such a way that anyone can see the data recorded on it. It is a kind of database in which the registered data comes to form a chain and moves according to the following rules:

- ✓ It is not possible to delete or modify the data enrolled in the network in any way. You can only add more data to the existing chain.
- ✓ Every time you add a block of data, the system performs a complex calculation to validate the process through the so-called "Proof of Work."
- ✓ Any changes you might want to try to introduce will be instantly rejected by the network.

With blockchain, it is possible to keep track of every transaction without them being manipulated nor modified in any way. The integrity of the entire system means that there is no need for intermediaries within the transaction, but that the traders have to trust one another without knowing each other. Blockchain is a decentralized or DeFi application, where no central computer acts as the authority for the network. Still, the power is distributed along with a peer-to-peer network, an architecture where all the computers involved act as both clients and servers. This system, created against information monopolies, ensures transparency of history while protecting privacy.

Encrypted art and blockchain are closely related. This technology allows you to create something digital that is perfectly equal to or more valuable than its physical equivalent. Blockchain-based non-fungible tokens (NFT) enable users to own digital assets outright. However, ownership of digital assets is fundamentally different from physical ownership because the digital assets or resources are kept in the digital wallet of the creator or collector. Then, the digital file, the token, cannot be reproduced as it exists as a unique code. In other words, to have a copy of the same work of art online, it is necessary to buy or create a new edition of it, for instance, a new token. It is defined, in fact, as non-fungible because of its intrinsic property that cannot be interchangeable.

An NFT introduces scarcity and its associated value within the digital context. Before the advent of blockchain technology, it was almost impossible to assign a value to digital artwork, given the possibility of duplication. But thanks to the blockchain and NFTs, a new market was born; that of crypto art. The blockchain or decentralized and distributed technology in which crypto artworks travel is Ethereum. Ethereum aims to develop smart contracts through the payment of an ether fee or EHT, which corresponds to the cryptocurrency. A peer-to-peer platform based on smart contracts, Ethereum was created in a programming language that travels through this network upon payment of a computational unit of account. In addition to being a cryptocurrency, Ether is also meant to be a fuel for operations and transactions from one wallet to another. During its transfer, and once the token has reached the destined digital account, the token remains the only copy, changing only the ownership of the artwork. Blockchain technology thus makes it possible to preserve the uniqueness of the digital information transmitted, and in turn, its value. The transactions take place in cryptographic form. Therefore, the only recognizability of the token, even once sold, is that of the author of the NFT.

What crypto art has managed to combine is the interest of young artists, both in creating works of art on a materialistic level, which includes drawings, paintings, and sculptures, and in the digital world, through networking and new technologies, such as blockchain. While blockchain can be used within many industries, it is in the art that it is now finding great buzz thanks to interested creators and investors who want to own something innovative and valuable.

An NFT can be anything, from a still image to a GIF, a video loop with or without sound, a song, and more. Once placed inside the Ethereum blockchain, these assets become tokens and can remain safe and inviolate, immutable, and indivisible. Simply put, the created file has become "tokenized," for instance, linked to something digital inside the blockchain, and tokenization is crucial to prove ownership of that particular asset.

At this point, the created token is not the artwork yet. Rather, it attests to its ownership. To generate the crypto art, extra information must be associated with the token, like a kind of metadata, among which is the link to the image, GIF, video, or song that you want to turn into NFT. Here, some doubts might start to arise. For example, you might think that once the NFT is created, the artist might modify the asset or that the host of the asset might disappear, but there are solutions for these types of problems.

The NFT is not the created artwork per se. Rather, the created token and asset represent the full encryption. So, even if someone copied the image, that copy would not matter because a copied item does not generate the same value as owning the original and certifying ownership. The ability to reproduce the image is not a problem for the crypto art market because it does not limit the ability to sell it; the NFT has an official artist value. NFTs indicate the official version of the artwork and revolutionize not only the way art is created, but disrupt the entire system of selling and buying as they can involve many more people, both emerging artists and investors.

Art and collectibles are a new and alternative type of investment. The value of NFTs is technically undoubted, but where is the value of a reproducible digital work, even if it is unique? Art is a personal thing that communicates with people. Even if you can't experience it firsthand, you can't touch it. Besides, some works tend to mark eras. Crypto artists don't just add pieces to the blockchain; they tell a culturally significant story of the technology itself as it develops. Digital galleries, like Nifty Getaway, Known Origin, and SuperRare, make a difference here as they pave the way toward experimentation and allow investors to support their favorite artists. Crypto art expands the limited opportunities to showcase and sell digital art at special events or gatherings on platforms. Besides, crypto art has the potential to expand the reach of digital artwork into the traditional art world, which is still hesitant to embrace digital art.

CRYPTO ART - BRIEF HISTORY

We are witnessing the birth of a new way of making art, creating community, buying, and investing. Although many have been exploring the concept of digital scarcity through the idea of selling art on the blockchain for quite some time, blockchain development is still ongoing. Traditionally, ,the general idea is that if something can be copied and replicated for free, its value drops; however, this market perspective now appears to be outdated in relation to digital art. Most collectors believe that for art to have value it must have a measurable and verifiable scarcity. Blockchain solves this problem for digital artists by introducing the idea of verifiable digital scarcity. Each artwork is associated with a unique token issued in the blockchain.

The first step in creating the crypto art marketplace was Joe Looney's Rare Pepe Wallet, which paved the way for the possibilities of buying, selling, trading, and giving away digital artworks on the blockchain. Joe and his community not only conceived of the first marketplace of its kind but were the first to prove that it could work on a large scale, selling digital art for millions of dollars. Rare Pepe Wallet were the pioneers of blockchain communities where anyone can buy, sell, and trade artwork, the first to offer these services without paying commissions, and the first to create digital artwork tied to the blockchain that changes its representation depending on where it is displayed, thus also proving that rare digital art can exist in the physical world as well. This was in 2016, and it followed another digital scarcity project on the blockchain that was related to online games, Spells of Genesis. The difference was that with

Rare Pepe, it was possible to create your own custom card and, thus, have a digital asset entirely of your own.

Rare Pepe was built on Counterparty, and in the wake of its success, we witnessed the birth of many other projects. Among the most famous of those is CryptoPunks, which allows you to collect avatars in low resolution and with different peculiarities, or Dada.NYC. These projects are very different from each other, but they established a model for the functioning of art in the blockchain. The thinking that has driven the revolution is decentralized ethics, which allow communities of artists to create a secure and profitable business model.

Once the opportunity to make money was understood, projects like Cryptokitties, based on Ethereum and allowing people to buy, collect, and breed tiny virtual kittens, exploded. After that, more and more blockchain-based projects were launched, and these became increasingly diverse. Among them are SuperRare, KnownOrigin, and DigitalObject. Although their offerings were quite similar on the surface, the artists and creator communities differentiated each project with their different approaches. The success of these galleries was initially due to the lowering of gallery commissions for primary sales and constant recruitment from below. Artists also began to tokenize their work in order to curate the presentation of their image on the blockchain, where they could curate both the look and feel of the user experience. This ability to take total control of the process also produced a gradual simplification of the tokenization process that led to an increasing interest in crypto art.

The art born with blockchain presents a whole new aesthetic and represents a new movement in the art world. Computers and the Internet have accelerated art's movement toward ubiquity and freedom, but through the blockchain, a digital artwork can now be as unique as the Mona Lisa. Thus, the process of liberalization has been reversed by reintroducing scarcity and authenticity.

CRYPTO ART - 14 KEY FEATURES

While no single crypto artist or crypto artwork can be uniformly defined, it helps to examine many common factors that have shaped the aesthetic and the community to date.

1- DIGITAL NATIVE

For the first time in history, artwork can be created, edited, purchased, and sold digitally and without intermediaries. A crypto artist can sell their work immediately, avoiding the long lead times involved in selling physical artwork and gaining many advantages, including the following:
- commissions on the sale are either low or zero
- can benefit from a percentage on secondary sales (royalties)
- has complete control over pricing and independently manages discounts or promotions
- is exempt from returns
- does not need to consider packaging or shipping
- can sell internationally without considering customs barriers or restrictions
- can freely exchange and give away artwork
- can capitalize on an existing physical artwork

In addition, any artist or collector can keep the artwork by storing it at zero cost in their wallet and have it available at all times to earn revenue. These advantages are already quite remarkable!

2- COLLABORATIONS

Crypto art platforms make it easy to tokenize digital and accessible art while also offering a new and attractive revenue opportunity. These NFT and crypto art marketplaces are also very inclusive in that they don't focus on an elite market segment but encourage emerging artists to create and earn fees.

One of the most notable aspects of crypto art is precisely the communities who gather around the platforms. Most marketplaces provide informal groups in chat apps like Telegram that allow for exchange and communication between crypto artists, collectors, enthusiasts, and founders in an unprecedented way. The groups are diverse and international and come from a wide variety of backgrounds, including developers, scientists, and artists. Thus, they tend to form truly multidisciplinary art collectives. What unites these people is the communal and inherently collaborative nature of the crypto ecosystem, an absolute abundance of innovative creativity, and the enthusiasm to imagine something different and push the boundaries of what's possible.

Moreover, crypto art is a new and dynamic market that inevitably attracts many disparate companies. This benefits artists who find themselves involved in exciting collaborations with brands that want to become part of the crypto world. For example, Pringles, the famous brand of salty snacks, has had a digital artwork created by artist Vasya Kolotusha: "Cryptocrisp," a 1080x1080 MP4 file depicting a golden Pringles can, is "the first virtual NFT flavor." The starting price for one of the 50 limited pieces offered on Rarible was about $2, and now, in less than a month, it's at over $2000.

3- GLOBAL

Artists from all over the world are participating precisely because of the blockchain's power and possibilities. This is why crypto art can be defined as a global movement with no barriers. With digital art, there are no longer any power centers, trend-setting galleries, or agents who make the best and worst of things. Instead, what matters is having an artistic verve, standing out from the crowd, and creating your own dematerialized place on the Internet where you can display your art and, thus, enter the market.

4- DEMOCRATIC/NO PERMISSION

Browsing through the online galleries, it is clear that everyone is encouraged to participate; there is no distinction among gender, class, age, creed, etc. Crypto art also redistributes power in the art market. Virtual galleries grant everyone access, like a kind of public museum. Indeed, blockchain and crypto art will change the way museums are enjoyed. For instance, even the Guggenheim Museum in New York is adapting to the new trend and looking for an expert in the field—not only to better understand the phenomenon that is overwhelming the market but also to intervene directly in the collection by planning an acquisition strategy and knowing where and how to invest. Museum executives have defined crypto art as "a fast-growing and highly desirable area for the art world." Will blockchain technology change the way museums define their missions, methodologies, and functions? The Guggenheim is among the first of major museums that are beginning to take the NFT topic seriously. Sotheby's has also recently chosen to enter the NFT market and set its sights high by betting on the Pak artist who managed to earn a million dollars with one of his NFT works in December 2020.

Finally, Phillips, another historical traditional auction house, has entered the great vortex of cryptographic art with the announcement of Replicator, a work by Mad Dog Jones that is able to generate new NFTs every 28 days. It's being auctioned off on the fashion house's website from April 12-23, with a starting base of $100.

Apparently, times are rapidly changing, and so are technologies. It's imperative to master virtual art and, potentially, make yourself accessible to the entire globe.

5- DECENTRALIZED

Crypto art is designed to reduce centralized power and increase the autonomy of artists. This allows them to break down the old canons of the art community and open up to an infinite audience without the need for intermediaries. In the traditional art world, intermediaries are galleries, dealers, auction houses, curators, and pretty much anyone who stands between the artist and a collector. For NFTs, intermediaries take the form of minting platforms. To create and sell crypto art, it is hypothetically possible to do everything yourself. What happens in practice is that you still need to become known and build distinctive and profitable personal branding.

6- ANONYMOUS
Every artist can choose to remain anonymous if they prefer. Anonymity allows for greater freedom from attacks or social criticism. Moreover, to cite Banksy's example, anonymity can also increase an artist's fortune by fueling people's curiosity. For some artists who defy government censorship, publishing work anonymously allows them to take advantage of privacy protection. The anonymity of cryptographic transactions, on the other hand, could create an environment ripe for exploitation, theft, and damage to an artist's image, which doesn't help with copyright protection. Want a concrete example? Works could be stolen and turned into digital tokens without the artist's consent. The 'theft' that many are complaining about is a classic digitization hoax. Physical works are copied, validated as NFTs, and then resold. NFTs certify the originality of a file, but they do not certify its authorship.

7- VIRAL
The meme economy is now a fact of life. Some crypto artworks are bound to go viral and welcome it because this allows them to spread quickly. This also changes the rules for art patronage and collection paradigms, making the principle of scarcity decisive in the overall outcome.

8- SELF-REFERENTIAL
Crypto art is a niche world where artists and collectors often find themselves quoting other artists or themselves or referencing key events and personalities in the cryptocurrency world. There are plenty of examples of this happening precisely because crypto environments are community-based. Whether it's on Telegram, Discord, Reddit, or other social channels, artists and collectors are constantly conversing and engaging with each other and generating debate. Thus, it is inevitable that they quote

each other within their works and are less referential toward more distant forms and modes.

9- PRO ARTISTS
Commissions and the costs of realization are drastically reduced. Also, each artist can obtain revenue from secondary sales through royalties. The advantages for artists are considerable, and it is interesting to see the birth and development of a phenomenon that allows artists to disseminate their art directly, establishing new relationships independently.

10- CHALLENGING TO EVALUATE
Crypto art is an environment that cannot be judged by traditional canons because these would kill the peculiarities and innovativeness of this type of art. For example, some of the criteria used in conventional art settings include the state of conservation of the work, the technique adopted, the support, the size, the participation in famous exhibitions, and more. These criteria simply are not applicable to crypto art. This is a new artistic expression that should be looked at with humility and curiosity, while taking into consideration that judging a work for its creativity, power of expression, and general artistic merit is highly subjective. It's important to remember that the purchase of a work also includes the emotions of the collector.

11- MATERIALIZABLE
NFTs are now a worldwide trend. Creators and collectors are emerging every day. Therefore, new products similar to digital displays or picture frames are being launched to reproduce their NFT artworks. Until now, NFT enthusiasts and collectors have kept their precious NFTs in a cryptographic wallet. Thanks to these devices, they are able to enjoy the purchased art by displaying it on the wall, like a real painting or video. The displays are integrated with major NFT platforms and have a slim design that can make the artwork or entire gallery of artwork stand out. No apps and no configuration are required; it's just a forever looping video or picture. With digital frames, you're not buying a gadget; you're purchasing a moving image that can be played back for entire days thanks to high levels of battery life. It is

interesting how the world of crypto art is forming a new art market and new interesting commercial possibilities. This market, we are certain, will constantly evolve in line with the needs of the artists and collectors who comprise it.

12- THERE ARE NO COPIES, ONLY ORIGINALS OR DIFFERENT EDITIONS

Collectors who purchase digital art own the works securely through Ethereum cryptography and can sell or trade the work when the demand for art is high. If a piece is sold or traded, the artists still have authorship attribution on each piece, ensuring that all credit ultimately goes to them. Although many have questioned the uniqueness of digital artwork, NFTs have reintroduced the principle of scarcity and renewed it. Today, even digital assets can be rare. From an investment perspective, it is essential to distinguish between single or multiple editions. In the past, multiples were a way to democratize the art of artists such as Duchamp, Picasso, and Warhol. However, in the age of the internet and social networking, artwork multiples present a new social value. With the generational shift in art collectors, the collection paradigm has also undergone fundamental changes. For younger collectors, the dividing line between fine art and trendy products has blurred, and exceptional works of art that truly stand the test of the market will not diminish market value; instead, those features only make the artwork more valuable. It's time to re-evaluate the principle of scarcity.

13- FREE ADVERTISING

Crypto art allows even the most emerging artist to make a name for themself. They can manage advertising through social channels—for example, Telegram or Twitter, which are the channels where fans are often found and where investors are also present. A crypto artist is often self-taught. This is a plus and a disadvantage if you don't have the technical skills to make yourself known and market yourself effectively.

14- VALUE OF THE ART = VALUE OF ETHEREUM + COLLECTABILITY VALUE

When considering the potential value of an NFT work, add these two crucial factors: the cryptocurrency used (Ethereum, for now) and the work's collectability value. The value of Ethereum is constantly evolving. For example, from 2020 to now, it has risen +1100%, currently arriving at around $2000. Moreover, some estimate that, thanks to interesting news for the summer of 2021, it may move towards $5000 by the end of the year, with an average of $3500. Warning: cryptocurrencies are highly speculative, volatile, and unregulated. They represent both considerable risk and the potential for multi-million-dollar gains. You need to consider this when entering this world.

In addition to monetary value, collectability value must be considered. A collectible is any item of interest or value to a collector. Collectible investments are typically "emotional assets," meaning that the emotional component—and often the hype that revolves around an artist, a work, or in this case a technology—make a difference in determining the value of an NFT artwork. People tend to want to collect what they have heard a lot about—something exclusive, sought after, and able to, potentially, make them rich. You could say that crypto art and NFTs move the concept of ownership and possession into a whole new field. We talked about the purchase of Beeple's and Grime's works at auction. Of course, "bragging rights" the right to brag about works that in reality are usable by all, but are in possession of the buyer only, are also significant. In crypto art, considerable curiosity and potential fame develops concerning the purchasers of particular works that have become trendy. The criteria used to determine the collectability value of traditional work do not fully cover the crypto world. They are evolving and yet to be discovered, meaning that they are often difficult to predict as well.

OPPORTUNITIES AND RISKS

Once the revolutionary reach of NFTs within the art market was established, a number of overlapping ethical, logistical, and environmental issues arose. Many people, especially artists and other members of the maker community, have pointed to the severe ecological impact that the explosion of ether minting and NFT trade will have on a planet already ravaged by climate change, climate-related disasters, inequalities over environmental exploitation in different parts of the world, and unequal distribution of resources. What do NFTs have to do with climate change? The process of NFT tokenization occurs by adding tokens to blockchains, which, combined with the surge of commercial transactions, including a huge amount of bidding and reselling, involves significant energy use. Ethereum currently runs on a paradigm called Proof of Work or PoW. The PoW algorithm is very processing-intensive, and with the rise in popularity of NFTs, it has become too big a problem to ignore. Multiplied to the nth degree, in a market driven by the desire to keep up, it has resulted in a new form of environmental destruction. Every transaction on the blockchain requires a transaction cost, called a gas cost, that corresponds to the computation that is performed and the computing power. It is estimated that a single transaction costs an average of 82 kWh, with emissions of around 106 lb (or 48 kg) of CO_2. On average, the expense of a single issue is equivalent to driving a gasoline car 1,000 kilometers. Moreover, a single NFT can generate several operations that can be classified as transactions: from minting (i.e., the creation itself) and bids when an NFT is auctioned, to transfers of ownership.

Much of the information regarding ecological concerns about NFTs stemmed from Memo Akten's important articles: "The

Unreasonable Ecological Cost of CryptoArt," Part 1 and Part 2, published in December 2020 on *Medium*. NFT art's offer of verifiable digital scarcity and proof of ownership is an unquestionable advantage, but it also comes with a significant carbon footprint. Akten pointed out that, for multiple editions, the figures are comparable to dozens of transatlantic flights. These results have overturned the optimism associated with the cryptocurrency market as a magical space freed from old gatekeepers and middlemen. As a result of her articles, a large number of grassroots movements have sprung up with the goal of zeroing out the energy waste produced by the NFT market. Artists, activists, and theorists are creating concrete responses and debates with the intent of generating a completely new politics of art on the blockchain.

Importantly, new opportunities arise from here. Led by Akten's example, many are moving to solve the gas cost issue, starting with Ethereum and other marketplaces like OpenSea. Ethereum, the platform that hosts the blockchains to which NFTs are anchored, is committed to moving to a more environmentally friendly form that also keeps systems secure and functioning—called proof-of-stake—but this has not yet actually happened. It is unclear when the change will happen. The constant research that takes place on these platforms is essential and must pursue a conscientious model. The NFT market is rapidly growing and unstoppable. A more ethical alignment will also help make profit more responsible through greater transparency. Moreover, the publication of data by platforms like Nifty Getaway will be able to help shed light on and expand the scope of the actual energy expenditure behind the crypto art market. In response to hard calls to address this problem, marketplaces say they can solve it in a few years.

HOW TO BECOME A CRYPTO ARTIST, STEP BY STEP

The time has come to delve into the actual creation of a non-fungible token. A crypto artist's goal is to create digital artwork to display in digital galleries and eventually sell in exchange for digital currency or cryptocurrency. First, you must create a digital artwork that comes from your own artistic expression and narrate the story of the creation process through social media or an article. Every artist needs to be able to share their creation experience to let people know about the work they are doing through special programs that can express their artistic concept. After that, you can dive in to the technical creation of the NFT.

STEP 1: CREATE A PHYSICAL WORK OF ART AND DIGITIZE IT, OR CREATE A DIGITAL NATIVE WORK.

One language designed for generative art is Processing. A JavaScript library that does the same things on the web is p5.js. Remember: every artist and every work of art has a story to tell. Share your story on Medium or sites and blogs specifically dedicated to the crypto world (for example, CoinDesk, Nonfungible.com, CoinTelegraph, Ccn, TodayOnChain, Bitcoinist, Bitcoin magazine, CryptoSlate, Null Tx, Daily Coin, and many others).

STEP 2: CREATE YOUR CRYPTO WALLET.

To create a work, you need to have a wallet. We recommend MetaMask for desktop or Cipher for mobile. MetaMask is known for being very easy to use and configure, but you are free to evaluate other wallets, such as the following:

- Rainbow
- Coinbase
- Enjin
- Exodus
- Trust Wallet
- Pillar

MetaMask allows you to quickly and securely access many popular NFT platforms. Moreover, you can install it directly into your browser in the form of an extension. To activate it, you will be provided with a private key (a kind of PIN to access your account) that you need to write down on a piece of paper and keep in the place you consider most secure. Without the private key, you will lose access to your wallet. Along with the private key, you will also be provided a public key (a kind of account number, if you're thinking in banking terminology) that you will be able to use when receiving payments or other digital works. You can create NFTs totally free of charge, without having to have any Ether in your wallet, but only some platforms allow it. In any case, putting Ether in your wallet allows you to better understand how it works; therefore, it improves your ability to manage it.

STEP 3 - CREATE A NON-FUNGIBLE TOKEN (ALSO FREE).

Minting platforms make it very easy to create NFTs. You can choose from platforms such as the following:

- Rarible
- Mintable
- Cargo
- And many others...

Keep in mind that many platforms allow you to create an NFT wholly free of charge, but just making the artwork and then adding material in Ethereum requires computing power and that power corresponds to a gas. Just like cars that need gas to move around, computers working on Ethereum require gas to move things around. Young up-and-coming artists without cryptocurrencies or looking for an ultra-low risk option can create NFTs on the Mintable platform.

Mintable allows you to create NFTs without owning Ether. For now, it is the only platform that will enable you to create a collection without paying any fee, but others are sure to be born soon. The transaction fee is paid at the time of your first sale. Registration is effortless, and you will receive a code via email to confirm your registration. At this point, you can start.

To create the token, just click on "mint an item" in the upper right corner. Then, you can create a new item or import one based on the token. By clicking on "create a new item," you can create your own NFT from scratch and for free. It is important to continue the process by entering a series of information about the type of token you will be selling, such as the title and subtitle. You can attach images, zipper files, videos, etc., of which an entirely customizable further description is required. Finally, you can set the price in Ethereum or set an auction with a starting price and a maximum time duration. Setting the category of the work is particularly important. Once you click on "List this item" at the bottom, the artwork interfaces with the wallet and notifies you that you are sending a transaction on the blockchain that needs to be signed through the wallet. Now that the token has been created, you can view the relative ID, which is the code relative to the creator, and the generated smart contract.

STEP 4 - SELL A NON-FUNGIBLE TOKEN

This is the most delicate part of the whole process. Even on Mintable, where you can easily sell your work, getting known is not easy, especially if you are a beginner. To enter and sell through the proper circuits, it is necessary to ask for exposure through popular galleries. Among the digital galleries, Knownorigin or SuperRare are two of the best, but you need to be selected to become part of their exhibiting artists.

In a short time, you will discover that selling works online is not very different from selling physical works. For instance, detaching yourself from a work created with commitment and passion is always difficult to overcome, even if the work is digital. The exciting thing is that once you earn your first ether, you might think of putting up your own collection on a platform where you can collect the works you own.

It is essential to keep in mind that some platforms allow you to set royalties on works sold. In this case, the percentage should be set at the time of creating the NFT. This allows you to earn money through secondary sales as well, provided that the royalties are transferable from one platform to another. The royalty system differs from market to market.
Remember to check periodically for offers to purchase your work. Be aware that offers can also be withdrawn. If, however, you are satisfied with the proposal, it is time to sell.

STEP 5: BECOME A PATRON (AND POTENTIAL FORWARD-LOOKING INVESTOR)

Consider donating your artwork and perhaps asking to receive artwork as a gift.
Feed the crypto market by investing in your own work, creating your own small collection of other people's work, or donating or investing in various projects to feed the world of crypto art. Promote it and make it known to a broader audience. Be an enlightened and generous patron. When you least expect it, this could be not only a noble and priceless act, but also a wise and disruptive investment that might change your life.

BEST CRYPTO ART IDEAS

However, before you start making digital art, you need to know the types and create something that is memorable and reflects your idea of personal art. There are various ideas to take inspiration from and techniques to experiment with in order to fully express your feelings and find the right path to channel yourself into this vast world of crypto art.

1- Digitized Art. Several artists have decided to tokenize their artwork. The introduction of a new, democratic, and innovative market has indeed intrigued the world. In his iconic example, Bansky, thanks to blockchain, digitized his work Morons (White) and then set fire to the original version, thus giving even more value to the uniqueness of NFT.

2- Collage. If you come from the 90s, you already know what we're talking about. Modern collages are created digitally and are an excellent way to communicate an idea, an impression, or an opinion. Style is created through images that are cropped and juxtaposed consistently with the artist's intent. This process also requires special skills in graphics programs and is a widely used and alternative art mode.

3- Digital Photography. Whether from a digital camera or smartphone or tablet, a digital artist can create effects that were once unthinkable. Photos can also be artistically manipulated to create different desired results. Digital images enable photobashing, which is the combination of multiple photos into one to make a realistic but impossible work that challenges the plane of reality.

4- Digital Painting. Digital painting can be both 2D and 3D and is suitable for professionals. You need a graphic pad and pen, and its purpose is to replicate the effect of brush and colors. There is also a type of automatic and fully digital painting called dynamic painting. The idea of art being released from human intervention is revolutionary and, indeed, a great source of inspiration.

5- Digital Illustration. If you are looking for a traditional but timeless art form, illustration allows you to explore and invent your own style rules. It is particularly suitable for those who want to experiment more with drawing using a combination of illustration and editing software.

6- Motion Design. Finally, many motion designers can start to take on the mindset of established and refined artists thanks to NFT. Digital sculpture comes to life thanks to motion graphics, and entire collections flourish. Motion design is for those who want to charge their art with good storytelling and communicate a message.

7- Pixel. This is achieved with low resolution images and is the style of the famous CryptoPunks, but with pixel art you can recreate images that recall the style of 80s video games, which had limited resolutions. This type of digital art is perfect for those who have a retro style reminiscent of Lego bricks.

8- Isometric Art. Although this form is stylistically similar to pixel art, it focuses more on the 30° camera angle that gives the impression of seeing three sides of an object at once. This type of art is more restrictive and with more precise rules from the worlds of engineering and architecture.

9- E-literature. E-literature or digital literature is cross-sectoral and still difficult to define. It concerns literature that is born and spread through the digital medium, including electronic poetry, collective novels, and interactive stories. It is a new way of understanding a very ancient art and is a perfect way to express one's vision in a mixture of image and words.

10- Fractal Art. Fractal or algorithmic art is a type of art that includes the use of mathematics. It is true digital art or computer art in that it is modern, generative, technological, and surprising. It is made through computational software that reproduces fractal images. It's perfect if you're a person with a unique technical background and love for math and want to declare to the world that art can belong to modernity and computers.

HOW TO SELL CRYPTO ART

Selling an NFT is not just selling the image, video, or GIF; it is selling a real digital asset. NFTs are often traded between marketplaces the way stocks and safe-haven assets are traded. Arguably, many people enter the non-fungible token marketplace because they hear of instances of resounding sales and intend to make seemingly easy money.

For an emerging artist who wants to be part of the crypto world, it's essential to know where and how to position themselves within the major marketplaces, but, most importantly, it's important to recognize that success doesn't come suddenly, even if it sometimes appears that way. It's made of constant learning, creativity, patience, and tenacity. Beeple, for instance, spent years developing his skills and building his community. Being a curious and resourceful artist can prepare you to best approach this new movement. Moreover, it's also imperative to understand that it can take a varying amount of time, depending on your personal journey, to study, learn, and experiment with NFTs before you start selling in earnest and see possible gains.

Either way, the key to success is to try. Focusing on the work and continuing to create art is imperative. What can make a difference is addressing a particular niche, a narrow and profiled audience, and creating something that is particularly suited to the interests and needs of that target audience. Create and deliver something of value. It's vital to not only think about the potentially passive and spectator audience, but to aim to create or be part of an active community that interacts, shares, and supports this new world. The largest crypto artist communities are mainly on Twitter, Telegram, and the leading dedicated marketplaces. They are spaces where you can exchange ideas and projects, promote yourself, and create new connections, opportunities, and inspiring collaborations.

Once you have taken these first steps inside the crypto world, it is time to devote yourself to selling your NFTs. First of all, it is advisable to tour the marketplaces and compare the prices of works to determine which range to position yourself in, keeping in mind that the gas cost, whether the buyer or the seller pays it, can sometimes be higher than the price of the token itself and that few still know about or have Ethereum to invest in crypto art. Several platforms are closed and work by invitation only. Others, which are open, like OpenSea, have gas costs that have to be paid when the work is created. To start selling on the principal platforms, you need to connect your wallet and make your NFT. You can create entire collections and, on some of them, set a percentage of earnings on secondary sales—i.e., royalties. It is advisable not to overthink these incoming costs, though, because uploading works to these galleries allows you to increase the value of your art for the simple fact that it is there and visible in a place specifically designed for that purpose and recognized as necessary by the audience. In addition, people are potentially more likely to spend substantial money on works that have been on display for longer on crypto art platforms.

Among the best techniques to succeed in selling NFTs, even though intermediaries are eliminated on the blockchain, is to have a good community on social networks. Social networks really work as intermediaries for the crypto art world. It is essential to create your own network of collectors to communicate new releases and sales. Gaining followers is not always a simple thing. It takes dedication, practice, and commitment.

Our primary tips for emerging in the world of crypto art are:
- Commit to joining and actively collaborating with a community of crypto artists.
- Stay authentic to who you are, what you choose to offer, and the message you want to communicate.
- Market yourself. Being a marketer may not come naturally to you, but make sure it doesn't hold you back. Learn how to make

genuine and meaningful connections with your audience, and you'll see the results.

Here are some of the most important tips according to crypto artist Trevor Jones:

1. Master your art form by continuing to study, learn, and experiment.
2. Build your brand by applying marketing skills at this stage.
3. Develop a recognizable style, and tell the story of your creative process.
4. Learn how to write a good press release, and get to know journalists in the crypto world.
5. Hope for the best. Prepare for the worst.

PROMOTE YOURSELF

To be able to sell, to emerge from the masses and make your fortune, the necessary skills remain the same: the artist must be known, as their signature may be more valuable than the intrinsic qualities of their work in a speculative marketplace. What varies concerns the marketplaces and sales platforms chosen. Traditionally, it was the galleries, with their closed systems and barriers. With crypto art, there are multiple platforms that offer alternatives and allow artists to leverage their personal branding on the web to gain an ever-growing audience. If an artist is able to promote themselves, as in the case of Beeple, they may find it easier to gain a following than in the traditional system. Competition in crypto art will increase in the future. That's why we suggest that you start now. To make your way on your own in this field, you need to know journalists, create genuine collaborations, write good press releases, and enter the circuit of artists. The most used channels are certainly Medium, to tell compelling stories about your artwork, or Twitter, where, in addition to crypto artists, you can find a good circle of collectors. An interesting alternative is community engagement on Telegram or Discord. However, Telegram remains the number one platform in terms of the number of crypto users. Therefore, it is advisable to create your own channels on these platforms.

Traditional art is based on its own rules, but NFTs are available to a potentially wider audience that includes the entire world. Marketplaces for artists have, fortunately, come a long way, facilitating user experience and improving their overall design. Usability is a crucial issue as far as NFT buyers are concerned. The technical tools are there, but the artist needs to expand and enhance collaborations, influencers, and their social media presence, all of which are valuable tools in the arsenal of an artist who wants to get known.

TOP MARKETPLACES

Each marketplace has its own philosophy, and new ones pop up all the time. That's why you need to discover them, learn about them, and choose the best one for your art and your style before opening your own gallery. The platform can also make a difference in establishing the value and popularity of your works.

ASYNC ART (HTTPS://ASYNC.ART/)
Async Art is a recent art movement built on the blockchain.
Within it, you can create, collect, and exchange programmable art. This is art that can evolve over time, respond to a stimulus, trigger a reaction from its owners, or follow an exchange price. You can purchase both "Masters" and "Layers." A Master is a 1/1 edition artwork, while Layers are the individual components that make up the Master image.
Layers come with special abilities chosen by the artist. When you edit something on a layer, the master image will reflect it regardless of who owns it. Artists pick the parameters of their art and grant exclusive control over each aspect to individual collectors. For example, they might enable someone to modify the state of the background, the color of the sky, or the position of a character.

FOUNDATION (HTTPS://FOUNDATION.APP/)
The particularity of this marketplace is that it is curated by the community. In practice, the creators selected only the first 50 artists, who then extended invitations to others and created the community. Invitations are limited for now. To become part of the community, it is advisable to make friends with members from whom you can then request an invitation—perhaps starting conversations with artists or collectors with common interests or

whose work you admire. Sharing their work on social media could be a great way to make friends and build a relationship. On February 19, 2021, the famous gif of the Nyan Cat sold at a Foundation platform auction for $545 thousand in Ether.

KNOWNORIGIN HTTPS://KNOWNORIGIN.IO/

To become part of the gallery of Knownorigin, it is also essential to be selected. The process of selection ensures that the works are of an acceptable quality and follow the philosophy behind the platform. Most of the marketplaces present themselves through Medium, through which they share their philosophy and manage a blog section dedicated to the major works in their gallery. Each digital artwork on KnownOrigin is authentic and truly unique. The Ethereum blockchain protects it.

MAKERSPLACE HTTPS://MAKERSPLACE.COM/

MakersPlace has been an active crypto art market since 2018 and is based in the United States. It is considered a high-value gallery.

The long list of creators with NFT sold on this market include names like Yura Miron, Silvio Veira, Dmitri Cherniak, Dreamonaut, and Frenetik Void, to name a few.

MakersPlace's primary focus is exclusive digital art, but it also features some less exclusive art. NFTs are based on the ETH blockchain. To gain access, you have to apply and be selected.

On MakersPlace, you have to pay a 15% service fee. We are not aware of any other NFT marketplaces that charge a higher commission than this, but a few charge exactly this (15%). There are also 12.50% commissions for any secondary sales on MakersPlace, of which 2.50% goes to MakersPlace, and 10% goes to the creator as a royalty. These fees are separate from the Ethereum gas fees that the Ethereum network requires to process transactions.

Every digital creation on MakersPlace is digitally signed by the creator and permanently recorded and verified through the blockchain. MakersPlace provides and manages a unique digital wallet for each creator.

MINTABLE (HTTPS://MINTABLE.APP/)

Mintable allows you to create NFTs totally free of charge by ensuring that the gas cost is paid at the time of the first sale. Mintable is a cutting-edge platform in which Mark Cuban has invested and which has auctioned the work of the 20th-century Ukrainian artist Wladimir Baranoff-Rossiné, whose works are managed by his descendants. The auction included an abstract painting from 1925 that had remained in the family since its creation and that was linked directly to an NFT on Mintable. In addition, nine digital representations of other Baranoff-Rossiné paintings, the originals of which the family will obviously retain ownership of, will also be sold with NFTs in three limited-edition auctions. This is a physical work certified on the blockchain by the platform itself. On Mintable, it is possible to buy and sell not only on the Ether circuit but also in Zilliqa with ZIL.

NIFTY GATEWAY (HTTPS://NIFTYGATEWAY.COM/)

Since 2019, Nifty Gateway has been owned by the Gemini Exchange company, founded by the Winklevoss twins, who are most known for their lawsuit against Mark Zuckerberg in which they claimed Facebook ownership. The platform's mission is to make the world of NFT accessible to everyone. On Nifty Gateway, you can buy, sell, exchange, and show so-called "Nifties" (name the platform gives NFTs). There are also various collaborations among the platform and the best artists worldwide, among which the famous American painter Micheal Kagan, one of the first traditional artists to approach the world of crypto art, stands out.

To sell your works, you need to fill out an application, make a presentation, and wait for the selection process. Once accepted, each uploaded collection will be open at a specific time (a drop) and will only be available for a limited time. New drops are expected approximately once every three weeks. After a collection's initial drop closes or runs out, you'll only be able to get Nifties from that collection in the marketplace. On Nifty Gateway, each time an artwork is purchased and sold, the artist gets a percentage of the sales. The artist can also decide on their own rate for secondary sales, which could be 5% 50%. Nifty Gateway takes 5% + 30 cents on each secondary sale to cover credit card processing fees and as an expense of running the platform.

OPENSEA (HTTPS://OPENSEA.IO/)

Founded in 2017, OpenSea supports NFT with ERC721 and ERC1155 standards. It is the largest NFT marketplace, containing over 200 categories and millions of assets. It provides a wide range of NFTs, including art, censorship-resistant domain names, virtual worlds, figurines, sports, and collectibles.

It, too, is open to anyone who wants to join, and you can add NFTs from different marketplaces. It has a rich blog section with the latest news and guides to create and sell independently, but the most inspiring part is the activities section, where you can keep an eye on all the latest offers and trends.

PORTION (HTTPS://PORTION.IO/)

Portion is an online marketplace that connects artists and collectors through blockchain technology to buy, sell, and invest in art and collectibles easily with total transparency. It includes the Artist Community, a global network of decentralized creators and artists. Here, anyone can be a collector.

You can control your physical and digital collection in one place, simplifying cryptocurrency exchange with art and collectibles. Portion tokens are ERC-20 resources on the Ethereum Blockchain, and members can govern and vote on the platform's future in a decentralized way.

RARIBLE (HTTPS://RARIBLE.COM/)

Rarible is a platform that is suitable for everyone, even beginners, and it's open, which means that you don't need to be selected to start creating NFTs on Rarible. Secondary sales take place on Rarible's marketplace; there are royalty options, and both single items and entire collections can be sold in bundles. Rarible is a community-owned NFT marketplace. Its "owners" hold the RARI ERC-20 token. Rarible awards the RARI token to active users on the platform who buy or sell on the NFT marketplace. Creators can use Rarible to "mint" new NFTs to sell their artworks, including books, music albums, digital art, or movies. Creators can also show a preview of their creation but limit the entire project to the buyer only. Rarible buys and sells

NFTs in categories such as art, photography, games, metaverse, music, domains, memes, and more.

SUPERRARE HTTPS://SUPERRARE.CO/

As with other marketplaces, to have a collection on SuperRare, you must go through a selection process. SuperRare focuses on being a marketplace where people buy and sell unique, single edition digital artwork. The team has to make sure that the works are original, created by real artists, and, most importantly, unique. On SuperRare, as anticipated, you can only sell single pieces and not series, and buyers have free access to the platform through MetaMask. Here, you can only use Ethereum for payments. The platform retains 15% of sales on the primary market and 10% on the secondary market for artists. SuperRare has also been chosen as a platform by *Time* Magazine, the famous American publication, which has auctioned three digital covers with the help of renowned entrepreneur, investor, and influencer Anthony Pompliano.

THE MINT FUND (HTTPS://MINT.AF/)

Networks like The Mint Fund, which cover the fees needed for artists to mint their first tokens, suggest that real-life social ties are being built that are far stronger than the blockchain. Mint Fund is a community project created with the sole purpose of building a support network for artists interested in bringing their art to the world of cryptocurrencies like NFT. The project aims to offer resources to foster a diverse community by allowing artists to coin their work simply by filling out a form. Art has the unique ability to highlight inequalities globally and shine a spotlight on ongoing social movements. That's why initiatives like The Mint Fund are born and remain essential to the development of sustainable and inclusive art.

HOW TO BUY AND INVEST

Buying crypto art is practically and technically quite simple. Once you understand how cryptocurrency and wallet work, what's left to do is choose. And for a collector or investor, this is a crucial step. Once you have purchased the desired amount of ETH through platforms like Coinbase, you need to connect your wallet to the platform where you want to shop.

Most marketplaces have an activity section that allows you to check the ranking of artists, and thus, choose the one that suits your tastes and what you want to spend. Besides, you can keep an eye on the artists who sell the most and on what kind of prices their artwork goes for. If you spot an inspiring artist, you can view their page and works, and then filter and sort the pieces from the lowest to the highest price. Otherwise, on the main page, you can browse all the creations within a price range that don't necessarily belong to a single artist. Once you have identified the piece you want to buy, you can either purchase it right away or make an offer for the amount you are willing to spend and let the artist decide whether to accept your proposition or not. The purchased piece appears in the wallet in about 10 minutes, following the creation of the transaction on the blockchain.

Getting started with collecting is quick and easy as well. No middleman is required. If you make an offer to an artist and they decide to accept it, the piece will be awarded to you. This process is fast, usually immediate, transparent, and secure. Once you have acquired digital ownership of the work, anyone can take the entire collection with them at any time. You can then give it away to whomever you wish across the planet, and storing the digitally encrypted work becomes much more straightforward than owning a traditional piece. Both primary and secondary sales are fully observable and transparent, but also completely anonymous if you wish. In the digital world, one challenge that is still considered impossible to overcome concerns the authenticity of one's work. However, today's platforms that sell crypto art in the form of non-fungible tokens have incorporated selling by selection. Selection allows for stronger input controls that will enable marketplaces to check that the artwork is authentic without preventing anyone from selling their art.

MAKE PROFIT

In the past, auction houses, billionaires, private collectors, and investors from around the world set the prices and values of works in the marketplace; these same interests will keep the NFT marketplace alive, active, and profitable for a very long time. Cryptographic digital artwork has immense capabilities, and it is inevitably taking over the world.

At present, solutions for issues regarding preservation, liability, and insurance are gradually being found. As new instances emerge, improvements are being created. This living market does not stop; it improves over time, intending to gain more and more respect, credibility, and recognition, especially with the general public.

Soon, collecting digital art will become standard practice. Moreover, while traditional galleries risk being left behind, there is a golden opportunity to invest in an emerging, secure, young, and dynamic market that generates value at an exponential rate. The timing is optimal for investing: tokenized art is cutting edge, accessible, and in step with the digital times.

Investing at this time is profitable for several reasons:

- It is the token itself that generates value. By creating scarcity for a work that is potentially accessible to all, it is the artwork itself that produces value for its buyer through circulation.

- Total NFT sales during a single month in 2020 were $250,000. Today, in the same month, the total reached $60 million, and the trend continues to move upward.

Profits will be huge and will increase because NFTs are not a temporary trend but a new way for modern generations to understand, conceive of, and collect art. Knowing the artists and following them on social networks allows everyone to verify their identity and achieve popularity. It is possible to choose the artists you are most interested in based on personal parameters or opt for those who break the rules and redefine a canon or those who have something to say and a story to tell.

If you still have doubts about investing in crypto art, just consider that the art market has always been resilient and has proven that it is able to renew itself and resist any collapse. Starting to collect today means being able to become, perhaps, a patron of the future or invest wisely to reach a higher level of liquidity in the not-too-distant future, given the speed at which new technological innovations travel.

LIMITING RISKS

It is not possible to know a world in depth without relating it to its potential risks.

One NFT risk is price fluctuation due to the number of people using the blockchain network. Each time you tokenize an artwork, you are creating a new block to add to the chain. To do this, a computing power is used that is expressed through a gas cost. More transactions simultaneously increase the price of this fee, and then the creation and sale of the work increase their value. The fluctuation of the value on Ethereum should also be taken into consideration.

Not all artists can afford to pay a high gas fee, which prevents them from expressing their art. In addition, platforms retain a commission on their sales, although this is not much of a real risk since platforms still charge a smaller commission than a regular art gallery.

A single Ethereum transaction requires the energy to power a computational network that eventually creates a new NFT and generates a considerable amount of CO_2. A frequently cited statistic from Ethereum's Energy Consumption Index pegs the average transaction at nearly 60-kilowatt hours or two days' worth of energy for an average North American household. This factor also contributes to the decrease in minted artwork, at least as far as artists who care about the environment are concerned.

NFTs took hold immediately, quickly, and competitively. On the one hand, they have allowed the sudden renewal of contemporary art, improving the outlook for digital art. On the other hand, they have attracted many reflections about critical issues that still need to be fully resolved. Thus far, the consolidated market is not particularly clear, so it is not easy to understand how to become a professional artist or collector of NFT. The crypto art market needs internal regulations to be developed in the meantime as this world continues to grow. But the growth is inordinate and fast enough to raise doubts and questions.

Beeple, who now collaborates regularly with Christie's, is building zero-emission routes by investing part of his revenue in renewable energy. Artists and marketplaces are the ones who will be able to change the direction and reduce the impact of emissions on Ethereum. One optimal solution is to replace the Proof of Work validation system with Ethereum 2.0's Proof of Stake, in which the systems chosen for the computational effort are chosen randomly and in fewer numbers. This could reduce the CO_2 emissions caused by the blockchain by up to 99%.

New projects are being created all the time that start from the bottom, such as Fractional, which allows NFT owners to issue fractional ownership of their works. Fractional allows owners to collect some of the cash associated with their asset without selling the work. It is a decentralized protocol that enables artists and investors to understand the marketability of the product. For example, selling a fractional piece at a price helps you understand how the market values that piece overall.

Fractional works through NFT vault, a sort of repository, which takes on the role of the custodian of the property and allows it to be fractional, after which the artist can auction, give away, or sell their fractional token. In this way, the ERC721 is transformed into an ERC20, then into a fungible token that can be traded and generate liquidity. Fractional artwork solves the liquidity problem of NFTs. This type of innovation is experimental and encourages the entry of implementations that are essential to ensure that risks are limited and the entire process is facilitated and secure.

SUCCESS STORIES

Morons (White), or Bansky the Provocateur

An incredible case of success for investors was Bansky's entry into the NFT market. The artist known to the world for his provocative verve has been at the center of a real market operation of incredible value. One of his creations, "Morons" (White), was sold by the Taglialatela gallery of New York to the decentralized blockchain company Injective Protocol for $96,000.

With a careful marketing campaign, the company tokenized the work on OpenSea and then burned the physical canvas by posting a live video on the Burnt Bansky Twitter account. In this way, the only original work with all of the same specifications and, therefore, recognized as an authentic Bansky drawing became the one on the blockchain. Injective Protocol could sell it for four times their original purchase price. This is a truly incredible marketing success that generated a lot public buzz.

WarNymph: Visual Art and Music at the Service of Success

The Canadian singer Grimes, also known for being the companion of Elon Musk, one of the richest men in the world, entered the world of NFT with a project called WarNymph Collection 1, which sold for $5.8 million and is already considered one of the most desired collectibles in the world.

Together with her brother, the artist combined visual concepts with tattooed cherubs and angels along with pieces of her original music and sold all 10 of her NFT works in less than 20 minutes on Nifty Gateway.

Very appropriately, some of the NFT reproductions featured cherubs and angels protecting Mars, the planet that Elon Musk intends to reach within a few years with SpaceX.

Those who bought these works did so with the prospect of seeing their value increase exponentially. WarNymph is Grimes's virtual avatar and has been used to promote her new album, and WarNymph Collection 1 is part of this fantastic promotional campaign. Thus, as soon as the album drops, those who bought the tokens will find themselves with an even more desirable object. And, if SpaceX reaches its goal, the value can be expected to soar. It is an exciting short- or long-term investment.

Homer Pepe: Art According to Generation Z

To understand the investment value of this work of art that sold for $320,000, you have to start far from the character of Pepe the Frog, which was created by artist Matt Furie and inspired several memes, including Rare Pepe.

In the wake of these highly successful memes, Joe Looney generated the card Homer Pepe, a collector's item that includes Homer Simpson in the guise of Pepe the Frog. This NFT was purchased for a price of $38,500. However, the seriality of the meme and its recognizability enabled it to acquire a significantly higher value. When the owner, Peter Kell, decided to sell, he did so at almost ten times its original purchase value.

Nyan the Cat: Virality as an Added Value

Also known as Pop Tart Cat, this work of art represents typical modern digital art, and its immediate virality showed the power of the Internet to share and transform different works.

According to creator Chris Torres, "Originally, its name was Pop Tart Cat, and I will continue to call it so, but the Internet has reached a decision to name it Nyan Cat, and I'm happy with that choice, too."

The value granted by the GIF's recognition and virality enabled the NFT to be sold for a sum equal to half a million dollars.

Bitcoin Angel or a $3 Million Mash-up

Trevor Jones combined his inspiration with the iconic sculpture of Gian Lorenzo Bernini in this NFT, and, in less than 7 minutes, he managed to achieve one of the largest sales in the history of non-fungible tokens.

By selling 4,157 versions of the Bitcoin Angel work at $777 each, the author made $3.2 million.

Collectors who decided to buy a version of the work now own an original that is worth much more than the original sale price if only for the fame it has acquired.

Everydays - The First 5000 Days: The Most Expensive NFT in History

The American artist Beeple, in collaboration with Christie's auction house, generated a total of $69 million for his work. The proceeds made him the third most expensive living artist in the world, increase the value of all his other works, and ensured his place in the Olympus of crypto artists.

The race to buy was tight, with Justin Sun, a digital entrepreneur, narrowly missing out on winning; his $70 million counteroffer, in fact, occurred as the auction was closing.

Beeple shows how the most enterprising collectors and the most famous auction houses are investing heavily in NFTs. Moreover, it reveals how, just a few years after their birth, these works of art have developed into a flourishing and creative market of extreme importance.

Jack Dorsey, Twitter, and Non-fungible Tokens

Jack Dorsey, the genius and billionaire inventor of Twitter, sold his first tweet for almost $3 million. As a demonstration of the interest of the market for NFTs, a Malaysian entrepreneur, Sina Estavi, CEO of Bridge Oracle, made the purchase and found himself the owner of the first message ever launched on one of the most famous social networks in the world. Some have compared this sale to having purchased a famous autograph.

Jack Dorsey's bet also ends with an even better happy ending, as the entire sum of the sale was donated to charity.

José Delbo, the Masked Superhero

José Delbo, born in 1933, is one of the most renowned comic book artists in the world, owner of some of the most famous drawings, and sought after by collectors of comics. Thus, when he entered the NFT market with crypto artist Trevor Jones, the web went crazy.

An oil version of one of the inked drawings of the dark knight, Batman, has been tokenized and put up for sale on MakersPlace for $552,603.98. The lucky investor will own not only an extraordinary collectible NFT but also the first official digital DC Comics artwork. This means that he will be the absolute owner of the work that marks the entrance of DC Comics into the world of crypto art, a record that will add even more value to this investment over time.

The New York Times Sells an Article: Art and Literature come Together

The article titled "Buy this Column on Blockchain" was written by journalist Kevin Roose. The article was sold on Foundation for $563,000, but it had been published in paper and on the web just the day before. The buyer became the owner of a piece of history that will never fade away: the first article ever to be sold as an NFT. In addition, the money was donated to the Neediest Cases Fund.

BEST INNOVATIVE ARTISTS AND THEIR PROJECTS

Beeple https://www.beeple-crap.com/

American Mike Winkelmann is better known as Beeple, a name so famous that it has become practically synonymous with success. His story is one of passion and a long apprenticeship. In 2007, Beeple decided that he wouldn't let a day go by without creating a work of art.

He started by drawing his Uncle Jim. Five thousand days later, the equivalent of over 13 and a half years, he became the creator of the third highest priced work of art sold while alive in the entire history of art, behind only Jeff Koons' Rabbit and Portrait of an Artist (Pool with Two Figures).

Everydays: The First 5000 Days is the name of the work in question. It is a collage of 21,069 x 21,069 pixels containing all the works Beeple created in those first 5000 days. Thus, there is a well-defined story behind the birth of this extraordinary artist who has been able to effectively represent himself and his dedication to his craft.

Blake Kathryn https://twitter.com/blakekathryn

Blake Kathryn is a visual artist from Los Angeles who works with the most important chains in the world from Adidas, Adobe, Fendi, and Facebook to Warner Bros, Columbia Records, and many others. Her artistic conception is so atypical and particular that she has been included among the most interesting and influential artists in the NFT field.

Her Venuses, women queens who rule the winds and seasons, have been sold on Nifty Gateway for over $1,500 each. The famous entrepreneur and heiress Paris Hilton, in collaboration with Blake, has launched "Planet Paris," her first collection of

NFT composed of three pieces already sold out on the Nifty Gateway platform.

Chris Torres https://twitter.com/prguitarman

If you associate the term meme economy with NFT, you can't help but think of Chris Torres, the creator of the gif "Nyan the Cat," a meme that sold for over $600,000. This crypto artist from Dallas, Texas created the gif in 2011, and it immediately exploded in a proliferation of shares and popularity. "Nyan the Cat" is, in fact, a network phenomenon of global proportions. PRguitarman, Chris's pseudonym, is the most shining example of a new reality that advances a unique concept of digital art that eradicates old concepts in favor of a fluid, digital, and hyperconnected world.

Dotpigeon https://www.dotpigeon.com/

Dotpigeon, a 33-yea-old from Milan, is notorious among crypto artists. When his works were auctioned on Nifty Gateway, they sold out almost instantly and earned him over 1 million euros.

His is an excellent story of victory. He worked for a web-based advertising agency while trying to break through as a digital artist. Now, his art is recognized globally, and he has decided to devote himself exclusively to that.

This artist, who wears a black balaclava as a rebellion against the social masks of bourgeois capitalism, is fascinating because he has been able to combine his skill as an artist with brilliant personal promotion. In fact, he talked about himself on Discord, presented at the Milan Plan X Art Gallery, and proposed that he be added to the Instagram page Larry's List, which reports the most interesting artists of the moment.

Giovanni Motta https://giovannimotta.it/

The Italian Giovanni Motta also represents the vanguard in the new and avant-garde world of crypto art. Born in Verona, this 50-year-old combines past and future in his works; his favorite protagonist is, Jonny Boy, the representation of his childhood self inserted into the digital world of NFT art.

After devoting a lifetime to perfecting his art, Giovanni Motta is one of the most well-known artists on SuperRare. He is recognized as one of the best-known names in crypto art, and his drawings, which are inspired in part by oriental culture and manga, explore the inner world of adults as they try to retain that fundamental part of their ego linked to childhood.

Hackatao https://podmork.com/blogmork/

Starting from solid experience with neo-pop and pop surrealism in the Italian market of tangible art, they were the first to tokenize art on SuperRare. The artistic minds behind the project are Sergio Scalet and Nadia Squarci. The real pioneers of crypto art in Italy and around the world, they are part of the beating heart of the digital exchange. They started by proposing an engaging and stimulating experience for traditional collectors and directing them toward the crypto art market. Compared to conventional media, with crypto art, they have experimented with a faster means of expression. Hackatao denounces the contemporary world's contradictions, and their art has an optimistic outlook that is wide open to the digital future in which they claim the right to express themselves without censorship or false idols.

Josh Pierce https://www.joshpierce.net/

Josh Pierce is a digital artist famous for his 3D NFTs. With over 100,000 followers on Instagram, he has become a protagonist on the world scene since his first appearance on Nifty Gateway. He defines himself as a visual artist and a motion graphics art director, and he focuses on themes that combine surrealism and naturalism, trying to create awe and spiritual calm by expressing the presence of spirituality in every present moment. His skill is the result of a long apprenticeship. In addition to being an NFT artist, he has also collaborated with the NFLLeague of American Football, Adobe, and multiple Grammy-winning artists.

Kevin Abosh https://www.kevinabosch.com/

The visionary Irish artist Kevin Abosh is linked to the IAMA Coins project and is one of the most inspiring and controversial digital artists. His turning point toward crypto art happened in 2016, when he sold a work of art that represented a potato for 1 million euros and was overwhelmed by the feeling that he had commodified himself. As a result, he decided to rebel against this by literally selling himself.

The IAMA Coins project binds 10,000,000 NFT works connected to 100 physical works by alphanumeric codes. The peculiarity of the whole thing is that these real works were made from his own blood. He literally tokenized and sold himself.

Incredibly active and always attentive to the current moment, he has created collaborations with other artists, inspired industry hashtags, and much more.

Pak https://twitter.com/muratpak

An example of personal storytelling, Pak is one of the most famous and well-known digital artists globally, earning the nickname of omniscient designer/developer/magician despite maintaining complete anonymity. Indeed, no one even knows if Pak is a single artist or a collective. Pak's identity is shrouded in mystery. What is known is that Pak is the founder and lead designer of the Undream studio and the creator of Archillect, an artificial intelligence built to discover and share stimulating visual content on different social media. Archillect is a real digital revolution because it is configured as a digital curator that, thanks to specific keywords, can search for images with minimal and aesthetically cold tones, in complete autonomy, without requiring external human mediation.

The auction house Sotheby's has chosen to collaborate with Pak for its entry into the digital world.

Pak is certainly not a newcomer, having been present in the digital art world for over 20 years, and is a compelling demonstration of how one must learn not only to tell their story in an original way but also be patient about developing their craft for the right amount of time before garnering attention. Pak's admirers include Elon Musk, the CEO of Tesla and SpaceX.

Trevor Jones
https://www.trevorjonesart.com/nfts.html

Trevor Jones is a Scottish artist who can claim a prominent place among digital artists who have linked their works to the blockchain. He creates digital drawings inspired by the great works of past artists and then animates them. His Picasso's Bull sold for $55,555.55, the largest Nifty Gateway sale since the platform's inception.

The artist is so famous that DC Comics chose him to work together with comic artist José Delbo and lead the publishing house's entrance into the world of NFTs with crypto art dedicated to Batman.

Xcopy https://xcopyart.com/portfolio/tagged/nft

Digital artist and cryptocurrency enthusiast based in London, Xcopy's distinctive and fascinating collections can be found on SuperRare and on Nifty Gateway. He maintains close ties with the entire community interested in NFTs, often delivering positivity and personal growth messages. Xcopy has become a true mentor to many.

His digital art investigates dystopia, death, and apathy through distorted images reproduced in a loop and has achieved extraordinary success.

NFT AND
REAL ESTATE

There is nothing more real in today's world than technology, and NFTs are proving it in a disruptive way. A universe no longer a niche whose sales have exceeded 250 million dollars and continue to grow day by day.

Collecting, selling but above all, investing and earning are the key words behind NFT. The capital is increasing more and more, and so is the interest in these products. How does an intangible asset that everyone can see achieve such value? How and who can create and sell their works in NFTs? What applications and results can they generate in the future? Is this a stable market in which to invest? Selling, collecting, investing, and earning, these and many others, are the possibilities that make non-fungible tokens a real technological bubble that is interesting and appealing to many. An interest that will not be extinguished and will find more and more market and uses. So many famous names have helped make NFTs even more popular. Non-fungible tokens are a unique resource of their kind. And in fact, everything about the interest and value of non-fungible tokens refers to uniqueness. What the non-fungible token creates is verifiable digital scarcity.

NFTs can be a revolution in terms of the many possibilities.

NFTS AND APPLICATION AREAS

Since Mike Winkelmann, aka Beeple, sold his digital work for just under $70 million, NFTs have become popular with the general public. More precisely, on March 11, 2021, at 4 p.m., what can now be called a true NFT mania exploded. NFT stands for Non-Fungible Token, which is a digital information recorded on the blockchain. These tokens are called non-fungible precisely because they are not interchangeable; they are unique and cannot be divided. What is special about NFTs is precisely their uniqueness and non-replicability, which makes non-fungible tokens so appealing. These tokens are cryptographic, meaning they represent something unique, such as a work of art, music, or any other collectible, and digitally certify ownership. Before NFTs, it was nearly impossible to authenticate and own a digital asset.

Although it is a phenomenon that exploded recently, it is impossible to say that non-fungible-tokens have just been born as their origins are actually related to bitcoins and the projects born to manipulate them. The history of NFTs is recent, and with many branches, it is still being written, and it is continuously expanding with a really huge turnover. The decisive year for the rise of the first NFTs is 2017, when Ethereum begins to increase its importance by announcing its own collection of Meme Pepe and then with the Cryptopunks project.

Non-fungible tokens today have branches in several areas, including:

• **Sports**. One of the first investors within the NFT world was Mark Cuban, owner of an NBA franchise, and since then, the world's top professional basketball league and several soccer clubs and many other sports have realized the importance of NFTs. NBA Top Shot is designed for true fans and collectors and is one of the first and most important NFT projects when it comes to sports. Owning in an unequivocal way an exclusive video of an action performed by your favorite player is not a small thing. Sorare, on the other hand, empowers you to play fantasy soccer, having the ownership of the purchased stickers and creating real teams. Sport with non-fungible-tokens opens to fans in a completely new and different way.

• **Fashion**. Digital fashion is today the vanguard of fashion, limited editions, and much more make possible unique fashion shows and collections and brings a high level of liquidity to a fast-growing sector. Digital objects, in the case of fashion, can be paired with NFTs, but that's just the first step. In the future, NFTs will make fashion.

• **Collectibles**. Collecting based on NFTs has its own backbone economy. It opens up to digital media in a completely different way than before, coming to meet the generations of the future. Under the name of collecting, different visions are brought forward: the desire and pleasure of interacting and owning unique objects or the desire to invest, collectors from all over the world love to own works of art whose value, over time, can increase and generate capital.

• **Art**. Art has always generated a lot of interest and is fertile ground for investors. Now that NFTs have entered the market, there is no turning back. Collecting is no longer the preserve of a single privileged class, auction houses no longer hold a monopoly, and digital artists have found a way to profit from their creations. The NFT era is a new era for art.

• **Gaming**. One of the industries that first believed in non-fungible-tokens and received significant benefits from them is gaming. The market was ready; gamers have always been familiar with buying and selling, and exchanging digital assets. The problem was that until now, they were buying something they couldn't really claim ownership of. The non-fungible tokens purchased now are verifiable and authentic. They create value for the players themselves and also lead to new forms of collecting; in this sector, NFTs are not just a trend, a fad but something that is already revolutionizing the market.

• **Real Estate**. The digital real estate sector provides a cost of production of land that borders on zero. Its true value is really connected to its uniqueness, to the fact of owning an asset or, better, an original and unique token. Here the convergence between real and digital has its highest expression. It becomes a thin line of demarcation, almost impossible to see. In places like Decentraland, it is possible to have your own store, with digital assets linked to a clothing chain and much more. Several artists have created NFT villas and collections to visit as well as huge virtual events. On these marketplaces, the value of a property or a piece of land becomes much higher than the real one, and a digital property is sold in a second without any need of a middleman.

● **Music**. From Mike Shinoda of Linkin Park to Kings of Leon up to Grimes, Elon Musk's partner, many artists are betting on NFT in a reliable and evident way. The first great passage from physical to digital music has been a lost race for many entrepreneurial realities that don't seem to have any desire to let this further innovation escape.

Create an identity identifier. Digitizing documents of any kind while maintaining their uniqueness is a unique method of eliminating the possibility of fraud and creating a digital space where individual identity is recognized and protected.

These and many other undiscovered areas are the fertile ground where these tokens are exploding, generating a multi-million dollar business. If the classic economy has always been based on the concept of scarcity to define the at, the network has undermined this concept. The web market is overabundant and disintermediated. For this, the NFTs are born to bring back the value of the assets of the market inside the Internet. With their own demonstrable uniqueness, NFTs are objects, works of art, music, and more that bring the concept of scarcity and perceived value of uniqueness into a world like the hyper-productive web.

There are many marketplaces where you can sell or produce your own tokens. Among the most popular and most used in different areas, there are Opensea, SuperRare, Nifty Gateway, NBA Top Shot, Sorare, and Rarible are just some of the most famous. Specifically for Real Estate, everything revolves around platforms like Decentraland, Superworld, and The Sandbox. We are witnessing the convergence of real and digital. This is because digital real estate has a cost of land production practically zero, and its value is linked to perceived scarcity precisely because it is NFT.

Today creating a store, a house, or any digital asset that can be connected to Real Estate is possible and convenient. Thanks to smart contracts, it is, in fact, possible to acquire and establish ownership of different digital realities. Thanks to NFTs, it is possible to own a digital house in which to insert virtual works, always in ERC-20, or to proceed like the big brands, which open virtual stores where it is possible to buy tokens of everything displayed there. Virtual events within Decentraland, for example, can be much more profitable and require less effort than real ones. Because of this, many companies realize that having a virtual store allows for staggering sales. Overpricing is often questioned when in reality, the value of virtual land is potentially higher: a Decentraland store and storefront will enable you to reach many more people than the same store on a real street.

Demand and collective confidence in the value of the virtual real estate is growing, and the change is happening fast. Another advantage of digital real estate is based on the ability to transfer ownership of the token and what is inside it in a practical and fast way. This transferability is much quicker and less expensive, and most importantly, does not require intermediaries. Transactions on Ethereum platforms are based on a transparent, unalterable, immutable, and unchangeable consensus mechanism.

It is the first time that users worldwide can create NFTs that these can be immediately available in marketplaces. Here people can buy, trade, sell and auction NFTs. The significance of this property lies in the fact that we are moving from sales within closed marketplaces to the possibilities offered by a marketplace that has an open and free economy. The ease with which users can create and then trade NFTs around the world through the blockchain is impressive and can bring many changes to the real estate industry. Transferability allows NFTs to be sold at a higher price than the real thing:

- Digital property can be sold in minutes without the need for a broker.

- Registration is self-contained.

- The property needs no maintenance.

Moreover, thanks to the smart contracts that regulate the transactions, each NFT provides a unique and non-falsifiable signature. The owners can then prove the provenance, making this type of purchase a more profitable and realistic investment. The virtual property built by contemporary artist Krista Kim is called

"Mars House" and is a property that sold for $500,000. Mars House has a design conceived by rounded lines and edges and furnished with fine glass furniture. Kim collaborated with musician Jeff Schroeder of Smashing Pumpkins, who composed the ambient soundtrack introducing the virtual property.

The owner of this virtual home receives the unique file of the project that can be uploaded to three-dimensional worlds like Decentraland and experience its augmented reality. An artist like Kim believes that the NFT real estate market can parallel the real one. Also, the home's furniture can be built in real-life replication by select Italian glass furniture manufacturers.

Real estate is notoriously slow to adopt new technologies. However, the very nature of real estate makes it ideal for blockchain applications: it is immobile and easily available to third parties with blockchain-based claims on it, such as collateral. The world of digital assets is expanding, and we are only now starting to see every part of daily life and business activities converted into a computer-readable format. Money is already digital; just think that only 8% of the world's currency materializes in the form of cash. Through blockchain, exchanges, transactions, and sales will begin to have fewer problems. Through the use of these digitized platforms, key stakeholders will see increased speed and lower transaction costs, along with an increase in available data. Transaction transparency, along with privacy protection, is essential when it comes to creating a healthy environment for buyers, sellers, and real estate agents.

NFT & REAL ESTATE: THAT'S AMAZING NEWS!

THE NEW FRONTIER OF VIRTUAL WORLDS

Many tangible items are now also coming to exist in NFT versions—everything from Nike shoes and NBA videos to crypto artwork and crypto kittens. Real estate is next. Virtual real estate represents the newest frontier of an already new market, and real estate investors from all over the world will not miss the opportunity to be among the pioneers of this new land. Wherever you are in the real world, you can log into a virtual world based on the blockchain. Moreover, you can access this virtual world through avatars that can occupy, buy, and resell entire properties.

It's not just about games: the popularity of virtual worlds like Decentraland and Cryptovoxels is expanding. In February 2021, a lot on Axie Infinity sold for $1.5 million before total virtual land sales peaked at over $6 million. This is a historical time and full of exciting opportunities for real estate. These metaverses are secure, and the smart contracts that handle transactions on the blockchain record and regulate every movement or property. Many people buy virtual homes to showcase their crypto art NFTs. They are basically art incubators hosting virtual galleries where they can have other avatars admire the properties they buy. The digital resources found in metaverses like Decentraland are part of a new kind of creative economy whose structure mirrors that of video games like Minecraft and Animal Crossing with the difference that in The Sandbox and Decentraland users can actually own the land they are building on.

Traditional practices have been turned upside down. The user can afford to do things that would not be possible in reality, such as interact with artwork. Virtual lands promise to transform and democratize the artistic experience, as well as the real experience. Anyone can enter a metaverse, acquire real property within it, and enjoy the rents on that property. Moreover, as the game becomes an opportunity, art enthusiasts have space to perform and continue expanding their digital horizons. It's a whole new world in which to participate, socialize, invest, and earn.

UPLAND: AN ALTERNATIVE WORLD MADE OF LLAMAS
https://play.upland.me/

Upland, a globally distributed platform based in Silicon Valley and founded by entrepreneurs Dirk Lueth, Mani Honigstein, and Idan Zuckerman, all started in 2018 during a game of Monopoly. The research and development center is located in Ukraine, where collectibles featured in video games based on blockchain technology started to make headlines in 2018. The combination of Monopoly and collectibles sparked the idea of tokenizing the real world.

Upland is a metaverse where people can play, but they can also socialize and, most importantly, earn money. For this reason, the platform is designed to be easy, understandable to all, and fun. It offers a virtual, augmented world experience and an opportunity for anyone to make some pretty good money.

Monetization on Upland is similar to a game that allows you to buy and sell real estate based on an actual map. The game screen is a little different from Google Maps, where you can move on real streets and view real buildings. This is a metaverse, an alternative world where you can buy, sell, and rent properties. The map displays real streets with properties already bought or for sale and the resources that users have placed within them, turning them into profitable activities. By clicking on a single property, you can place your avatar in the area, find game clues, or see it live, but the real purpose of the game is to manage the purchased properties and resell them to the highest bidder. The game also includes rent collection and credits that accumulate for each action taken, and these can be spent to obtain information about a home.

Upland's blockchain allows you to:
- have a secure record of every transaction;
- trade on a decentralized platform with no transaction fees; and,
- exchange tokens for traditional currencies.

In partnership with Tilia Pay, Upland launched the first virtual trading asset for NFT in fiat, still only in USD, becoming the first platform to exchange virtual properties for cash. Thus, the game became very serious.

MARS HOUSE
https://vimeo.com/416558553

Real estate, digital, and art meet dematerialization in the cosmic void under the roof of Mars House, the hyper-futuristic house designed by Krista Kim and sold exclusively on SuperRare, in Ntf, for 288 Ether, the second most valued cryptocurrency, for now, after Bitcoin.
Is the future of real estate really here?
Let's just say it's an exciting and profitable opportunity for the industry.
Returning for a moment with our feet on Earth and trying to understand, as mere mortals, what happened, we can rewrite the story as follows: the space-accented villa, virtually designed by the artist who founded the Techism Movement, was purchased by the collective "Art On Internet" on the revolutionary platform dedicated to the trading of digital works of art for a sum equaling $ 514,557.79 (about 431,000 euros).

The house is there but does not exist: it's all true.

The paradox of the phantom purchase melts away as soon as you understand the potential of Nft.

Let's imagine for a moment the Ntf as if they were dematerialized bricks. Everything they realize is intangible but purchasable. There is no property address, but the owner can exist. "As a Techism artist - a movement that reconciles technological innovation with creative inspiration - I am challenging the power Nft as an artistic medium," said Krista Kim, the South Korean-born Canadian founder of the Techism Movement. "Mars House will live forever as Nft."

The house, which goes beyond traditional architectural design and involves the canonical approach of a work of art, is a concept born from an idea that emerged during the pandemic. Space knows no limitations. Like a virtual canvas, it is an empty place to be filled and bridged.

A small piece of history in the real estate market, the Mars House is the first home ever sold this way.

As previously stated, when digital content is sold through Nft, it doesn't become visible only to its owner but remains available on the web. Therefore, to discover the Mars House, all you have to do is find it on Vimeo.

You will find yourself afore a clip of almost three and a half minutes, with a strong digital zen atmosphere, the result of Kim's collaboration with Jeff Shroeder, guitarist of the Smashing Pumpkins and creator of the musical base.

However, art on the Internet will also offer the possibility to share the concept to a metaverse, a 3D immersive world, to live it through virtual reality.

Located among the Martian heights, the dwelling is about as futuristic as you could dream it to be. But patience; if theoretically transferred to the real world, it would be challenging - if not impossible - to achieve. What primarily strikes us, in fact, is the absence of load-bearing walls holding the roof — an unusual but necessary renunciation, given the artist's desire to "create a meditative environment on our screen, like a digital Zen garden." Therefore, it is easy to understand how instead of - internal and external – walls, there only are continuous and transparent glass windows. In brief, space appears to know no limits, thus promoting the expansion of the consciousness of those who inhabit it.

The interiors
Another peculiarity is the presence of only two rooms inside the house: a spacious living area with a huge curved sofa and a large dining table that stands out, and a bedroom with a double bed. There is no bathroom nor kitchen. Even the furniture, modern and essential, also seems to be made of glass. "They can be made both in reality by Italian glass furniture craftsmen - reads SuperRare - and visualized through the technology of MicroLED screens." But there could also be sufficient room for a corner dedicated to digital art: "Everyone should install in their home a led wall for Nft art," said Kim. "This is the future, and the Mars House shows the beauty of this possibility."

The swimming pool
Outside, find out the fantastic infinity pool with sun loungers and sofas for sipping a drink by the water. However, getting into a bathing suit would require Wim Hof's tolerance to the cold. Indeed, temperatures on the planet range from as low as -140°C in winter to as high as -14°C in summer. What's nice, however, is the possibility of illuminating the entire area with different colors through the lamps located inside the apartment.

Solidarity aim
Beyond its artistic value, it is essential to underline the solidarity purpose of the initiative. Kim and Schroeder have decided to allocate most of the proceeds from the sale of the Mars House to their Continuum Foundation. This organization will support a world tour of sound and light art installations to heal and improve mental well-being. "We want to remind future generations that we are here to create a new and better world," they said.

FLYING IN COLORS
A REAL HOUSE BECOMES AN NFT
https://dulgeroffnft.com/

Shane Dulgeroff, a brilliant and innovative American real estate agent, had a revolutionary idea: to sell the house located at 221 Dryden Street in Thousand Oaks, California, as an NFT. Thus, he put the house up for auction on the OpenSea marketplace. The idea is to use a virtual, decentralized platform to sell a real, physical property. Shane Dulgeroff is an innovative specialist and investor in the luxury real estate industry. His goal is to intercept real estate investors and stay on top of the market and its trends. He intends to explore new territory in the real estate industry. Exciting videos on Dulgeroff's website accompany the entire transaction, introducing the home to potential buyers.

The home is complete with a garden and pool and features two bedrooms, a kitchen with state-of-the-art appliances, a bathroom, and wood floors. It is not the home that has been tokenized; rather, an NFT of crypto art named "Flying in Colors" is available on OpenSea. The designer of the NFT is established crypto artist Kii Arens, who has worked with the likes of Lady Gaga, The Rolling Stones, Dolly Parton, Radiohead, and many more. With her art Arens, expresses her idea of the concept of home: the animation represents a lunar, pop vision of home and is a true work of crypto art with a digitally replicated view of the San Gabriel Mountains.

Shane Dugleroff's idea is to bridge the gap between the real and the virtual by having both interpenetrate. On the site, there are also documents about the house and the guide to buying the NFT. This is a real estate deal absolutely worth testing now that the market is still a bit undefined in terms of taxes and regulations specific to a sale of this type. The NFT video of the house is tied to the real property of the house so much that it is not possible to split the two properties. Moreover, Dugleroff has simplified the process of accessing real estate by bringing it to the attention of younger people and expanding toward an entirely new audience: digital investors.

Dulgeroff's initiative encountered some issues that caused the deal to fall through. Among them, we find three crucial considerations:

1. Potential NFT buyers faced a hurdle due to the additional costs involved when purchasing an investment property versus a purely digital asset. Indeed, even though it is connected to an NFT, the purchase of any real property has significant legal and tax implications for the buyer.

2. The gap between the two investment worlds that Dulgeroff sought to bridge was much more significant than he expected. That's because, behind the offering, there has to be a buyer who equally understands cryptocurrency and NFTs and the real estate market and property management. This requirement made it much more difficult, at least for now, to find an audience for the investment. The end-user of NFTs is a precise target audience because some purchases are aimed at a life in the digital wallet, and then, within the blockchain. Therefore, as a house needs proper maintenance, it is an entirely different investment.

3. Limiting yourself to crypto buyers still means cutting off a substantial portion of the real estate market.

However, we are confident that his attempt is promising and allows those who want to experiment creating real opportunities in the field to take advantage of the strengths and weaknesses brought out by Dulgeroff, who is looking for the best strategies to make this new market a disruptive and profitable innovation.

REAL ESTATE: NOT ONLY LUXURY BUT ALSO AFFORDABILITY WITHIN EVERYONE'S REACH

The news circulating on the Internet about the great sales and investors' interest in the NFT world make it seem like a sort of golden mystique has been created around it. This is not entirely true. The NFT world is open to everyone, and this initiative proves it. The non-fungible-token world is cloaked in a shiny aura of luxury and glitz, but this is only a partial view. NFTs open the door to unparalleled democratization in investing that is impossible anywhere else. It is by following this principle that blockchain platform Enjin and LABS Group have begun a collaboration that opens the door to low-cost, affordable real estate investments.

Fractioning high-yield properties such as luxury apartments, villas, and hotels in the form of tokens will allow small and micro-investors to enter a market hitherto precluded to them while also providing additional benefits that ultimately open to a new era in the real estate market. Transactions processed through Ethereum will allow both buyers and owners of large real estate assets to cut down on the high costs of using third parties and eliminate the long waiting times due to national and supranational regulations.

The tokenization of small fractions of prime real estate will allow for a large infusion of liquidity into the global real estate market, creating the largest asset class in the world with an estimated value of $228 trillion.

NFTs created through Enjin will be integrated into the LABS Group's platform, where only approved property owners will be able to coin their own NFTs. All of this will be protected by both the inherent properties of the blockchain and the LABS Security Exchange regulation.

With a price tag of only $100 per fraction of NFT, anyone will be able to invest in and hold ownership of a portion of a luxury resort, hotel rooms, and even entire buildings. Investors will be able to store and manage their real estate assets within Enjin's blockchain wallet and verify the ownership, origin, authenticity, and uniqueness of the digital NFT, which is a unique way of combining the real and the digital to create a democratic win-win system. Investors will be able to boast ownership of a portion of a luxury property by sharing dividends, while real estate developers will have the opportunity to create liquidity.

862 FENIMORE, NEW YORK: ART AND REAL ESTATE MEET THANKS TO NFTS
https://www.862fenimore.com/

The house listed as NFT on OpenSea on April 8, 2021 is not simply a home but a work of art created by the famous American architect Paul Rudolph, founder of the prestigious Saratosa School of Architecture and deus ex machina behind the construction of legendary buildings around the world. Rudolph worked on this project throughout the 1980s, planning additions and improvements that would make the building a truly timeless jewel.

Today, this rare historic building has been remodeled under careful supervision to keep the original idea intact. Solar panels, ecological foam, and geothermal systems were added to make the house a zero-emission home while implementing all the amenities of 21st-century luxury. Thus, the home of the future is a 9,000-sq ft. historic building on 2.49 acres of land.

The innovation of the project is that with an auction base of 1 Ether and a reporting fee of 2%, it is possible to access the auction and win the NFT of this building of absolute prestige whose real price, as quoted by the Paul Rudolph Heritage Foundation and the Paul Rudolph Foundation, would be impossible for most people. In this case, tokenization enables an extraordinary opportunity because whoever wins the auction will own the NFT and the real property connected to it.

Whoever wins "The World's First Art as Architecture NFT," in addition to owning a unique piece, will also receive ownership of the physical house represented by the enclosed:
- Certificate of ownership of the physical residence
- Possession of all control systems connected to it
- All appliances and furniture in the home

In an unstoppable process, the blockchain and the world of non-fungible tokens are interacting with and interpenetrating physical reality thanks to the possibilities of real estate. New investment possibilities that were previously impossible to imagine are now opening up and promising to change the world of the global real estate market.

NFT REAL ESTATE IN SAN FRANCISCO

Jered Kenna, founding entrepreneur and CEO of 20mission Co-living/20mission Cerveza, is auctioning off a rather substantial NFT: the rights to a 75-year lease in his 20Mission co-living space, paid in the form of an NFT. Whoever wins the auction will pay $1 a month and no utility fees for the co-living space in a 41-unit building in the Mission District, where tenants regularly pay up to $2,200 in monthly rent.

This innovative project will tokenize physical rather than virtual properties for the first time, thus revolutionizing the real estate industry as there is no direct precedent for an NFT lease. And in the wake of Dulgeroff, the real estate agent who tried to sell a property by associating it with a piece of crypto art in NFT, this initiative explores another direction, envisioning a long-term project. The famous Bitcoin house auctioning off the lease is located in the heart of the Silicon Valley startup community. In addition to the lease, the auction winners will receive an additional

NFT that gives them the exclusive right to use the purchased space as a virtual asset.

Developed by Jered Kenna, Bitcoin exchange pioneer and founder of the first Bitcoin exchange in the United States, 20Mission is a cryptographic landmark of the very first Bitcoin house. It hosted the first San Francisco Bitcoin meetups, the first Bitcoin art show, and was also the site of the first documentary about the currency, *The Rise and Rise of Bitcoin,* released in 2014.

20Mission owns luxurious co-living spaces located in the heart of San Francisco and fully equipped for living with a built-in startup community aimed at fostering entrepreneurship. Together, these commercial spaces and individual rooms represent a 41-room community geared towards art, technology, and entrepreneurship, and located in the center of the Mission District. For this reason, Kenna's is a potentially winning strategy as it aims to attract numerous investors and young people interested in projects like this one, who will become the tenants of the home and will not have to pay additional taxes for it.

Jered Kenna is striving to replicate the success that NFTs have encountered while selling virtual properties by introducing a completely new model that can disrupt the real estate market. It's a sizable bet worth monitoring. The building has intrinsic value for its historicity and influence. Still, it is considered a suitable investment property whose rental appears to be facilitated and made more fluid and convenient for everyone.

QBC ENGADINE SA: THE TOKEN BUSINESS

Qbc Engadine SA is a newborn, St. Moritz-based company with a very ambitious goal: to simplify the bureaucracy associated with the transfer of ownership of various digital assets. The business is linked to the Quantico Business Club, an exclusive group of entrepreneurs that offers its members assistance, know-how, and confidential networking to create new business opportunities. Already very active in the growth of SMEs, this reality is now introduced to NFT investments with Qbc Engadine SA.

Qbc Engadine was created to buy, sell, and manage real estate assets sold in the form of cryptographic tokens. This company's first project will consist of distributing and making the building's property with six apartments saleable via blockchain. Leading the project will be the administrator, Gianluca Massimo Rosati, well known for his tax escapology techniques and ability to make transactions between companies fluid and secure.

Also part of the project are strategic partners:

- The Great Living Estate, an agency specializing in the search and renovation of prestige and luxury properties;
- Luxochain, an agency active since 2017 in the production of NFTs that will lead the tokenization process;
- Terrabitcoin Club, a club of large crypto investors.

The company was created to take advantage of the great ferment around NFTs and the legal benefits of transactions through cryptocurrency, which can count on a more streamlined, more accessible, transparent, and secure real estate sales system.

10 MILLION EUROS AVAILABLE FOR DIGITAL ASSETS

German stock exchange operator and security exchange platform Deutsche Börse, along with German bank Commerzbank, have invested in a new platform called 360X, which aims to create new markets for digital assets. For now, 360X focuses on supporting investments in art and real estate.

Thus, banks and credit institutions are taking over the virtual real estate and crypto art markets to support the trading of non-fungible NFT tokens. Carlo Kölzer, founder and CEO of 360X, said they selected art and real estate because, historically, both have proven to be illiquid markets. 360X's goal is to make many more things investable. And to do so, the German company has invested as much as 10 million euros for a roughly 50 percent stake in 360X, while Commerzbank owns a smaller share.

Kölzer and his colleagues had already worked together when founding 360T, an electronic foreign exchange platform, in Frankfurt, in 2000. Meanwhile, Deutsche Borse and Commerzbank experimented with blockchain technology in 2019. Now, with more experience and a vision axed on the future, they are ready to enter the NFT field. The real estate market is resilient and constantly changing, has been able to withstand disastrous inflections, and always supports good money circulation. The virtual real estate market appears leaner, faster, agile, able to allow incredible earning opportunities, and has a smoother and simplified management of national and international rules since the exchange of digital assets in blockchain follows the rules of smart contracts.

HOW MUCH CAN A VIRTUAL REAL ESTATE PROPERTY BE WORTH?

When we talk about NFT, we often talk about records. Well, even in the field of virtual real estate, a record has been broken thanks to a game, Axie Infinity, a universe of tokenized digital animals in which players fight, care for, mate with, and exchange fantasy creatures called Axies. Again, this is a game to be taken seriously, and many have long understood this. The sensational purchase concerns as many as nine blocks of Genesis land for the sum of 888.25 ethe (although the currency in the game is called Moon), which is equivalent to $1.5 million. This transaction represents the largest ever NFT transaction of Genesis land, which is highly valued property due to being rare and better placed in the game.

The "lands" on Axie Infinity allow you to generate infinite resources. Owning land in this metaverse is already very rare, as all lots have now been sold. Thus, the possibilities of gain for those who are active on the platform multiply exponentially. If you own a lot, you can build structures on it, create potions or other resources that can be used in the game, and acquire a decisive role by placing features such as rivers or roads in your lots.

In this game, the sale of virtual lands is a real event offered in the form of an auction, and every single quadrant of land contains trunks and treasure chests that enrich the user's experience. Located in the center of the map, Genesis land is scarce, as it is limited to 220 plots. Activity in the virtual lands, incentivized by a system that rewards users with fantastic new experiences, involves more showing off than playing. This game allows you to make virtual real estate purchases and acquires value based on the players' consent. The value of virtual appreciation is increasing by leaps and bounds, and the real estate industry should take advantage of this digital renaissance. Axie Infinity also plans to launch an interactive system called "Project K" that will allow players to explore, decorate, fight, and collect resources on their virtual land. In addition, the platform is constantly being revamped, even allowing players to bypass the considerable gas fees thanks to the Ronin sidechain developed by Sky Mavis and installable as a Chrome extension. Moreover, there are many other exciting projects in sight, such as the development of Android and Apple apps.

NFT & REAL ESTATE DISRUPTIVE PROJECTS

AXIE INFINITY
https://axieinfinity.com/

This game involves users taking care of small pets, very similar to Pokémon. These pets are designed to socialize, fight, accumulate points, get improvements, and reproduce. Another interesting thing you can do on Axie Infinity is buy land and own your own home. Axie Infinity animals move on the blockchain and are made according to ERC-20 tokens—i.e., AXS, the platform's native token.

In games based on the Ethereum network, you can successfully earn cryptocurrencies or contribute to the ecosystem by creating value. You can develop these properties over time and upgrade them. This world was launched in 2018, and all game actions have always been registered on the Ethereum network. Each tiny animal has its own characteristics and abilities in combat, and each of them has been able to gather communities around them that are enriched daily with new players. Although it is taken for granted today, at the time of its arrival, Axie Infinity's ease of use and infinite possibilities revolutionized game play. Today, it is constantly evolving while remaining reliably based its original features.

In 2020, the game became part of Binance Launchpad, which ensures the development of the entire game economy and acts as its support by accessing a centralized exchange platform. Binance Launchpad is a feature of the platform that allows tokens to be launched on Binance. Startups that want to develop their own tokens here can do so by leveraging the Binance brand to gain notoriety. At the same time, investors are assured that the platform has done extensive research to ensure the reliability of the company.

Due to the high investor traffic, the platform has created a lottery to keep the whole service fair. To participate in the lottery, you need lottery tickets. The tickets are given out according to how many BNB are present in the wallet. If you are chosen during the lottery, you have the opportunity to acquire tokens and tokens of the start-ups. In the marketplace on the site, you can see the volume that the game has generated. In the marketplace, you can buy characters and lands divided into different classes. Pairing, reproducing, and making the game characters evolve means having a real possibility of increasing the value of and then selling your tokens. That's why it's crucial to understand how the game works.

The collectible creatures have different powers and abilities to be acquired and enhanced. Their fight takes place within the land, which is called precisely "land." The combat takes place on turns, and the power of these tiny monsters resides in the various parts of their bodies, such as the mouth, the tail, the back, and the horns. It is these characteristics that determine the statistics and abilities that you can use. Axie organizes events and tournaments to give out prizes. The contests celebrate essential partnerships such as the one formed in 2020 with Ubisoft Entrepreneur Labs. The landscape plays a significant role in the game. Lunacia, as the world of Axie Infinity is called, is composed of four types of land:

- Savannah
- Forest
- Artic
- Mystic

There are also special lands, such as Genesis land and Luna's land. Each land contains placed items and resources, and each land type grants skill boosts to little Axie. Lunacia consists of tokenized land appreciations that can be sold, bought, and rented by players. The owner can customize the land to house stores, markets, or crucial points in the game within their land, such as dungeon entrances. The possibilities are truly endless. For instance, they can host structures and expand them over time or generate new resources that can be used, sold, and traded. As of today, land lots are finite. The only way to get new land is to make in-game purchases. The real estate sector cannot fail to take advantage of this historic moment: the land of Axie Infinity has a monetary, social, entertainment, and economic value not to be underestimated.

CRYPTOVOXELS
https://www.cryptovoxels.com/

I n 2018, Nolan Consulting, an independent game developer based in Wellington, New Zealand, created Cryptovoxels. Initially a project to build a simple metaverse, the author saw its possible expansion via the Ethereum blockchain using a standard ERC721 token. Cryptovoxels is a Minecraft-style game but represents much more for real estate investors and users as it enables:

• The e-commerce of land, property, and more. Cryptovoxels allows users to truly own their items and the digital assets put in place. There, you can buy and sell lands, objects, artwork, and much more.

• A wholly social world. It creates a space for sharing and socializing.

• Creative space and a video game. Cryptovoxels is a world created by users and editable by them. You can create stores, pubs where you can play, recording studios, art galleries, and anything else you can imagine.

The game's interface is very intuitive, which seriously expands its investment possibilities since it looks like a user-friendly virtual reality platform. Indeed, once users have connected their metamask wallet to the game, they will have an avatar, to which they can give a name and buy wearable devices. Once done and after buying land, they will be able to start building whatever they want and wander freely around the city, buying and visiting places like in the real world. Although at this time, Cryptovoxels is mainly used as a base for virtual galleries of NFT and virtual conferences in augmented reality, the possibilities for economic expansion are numerous, hence why the lands in Origin City are all sold out.

The developers have thus announced the opening of Proxima Tower Island, a tower island connected to Origin City by a bridge, where it will be possible to buy an apartment rather than land. The 80 apartments are for sale at $200 each, a much lower price tag than land in Origin City. They are being targeted by real estate investors who have understood the potential of a booming world, where you can buy and sell without the restrictions of international laws. Nolan has created a sandbox on the island, where you can now build your own objects without owning a parcel.

Cryptovoxels is a world in full expansion. A point of connection between investors, artists, auction houses, brands, and companies looking for a place of lasting interactions with the public, now that virtual reality for users is closer than ever to the real world. Investing in land in virtual worlds, like this one, means opening the doors to the digital innovation of the metaverse, which is increasingly conquering future generations and positioning oneself at the forefront of a lively and decidedly remunerative market.

DECENTRALAND
https://decentraland.org/

D ecentraland (MANA) presents a virtual-reality platform based on the Ethereum blockchain. With it, users can build applications and content while generating revenue.
It is the first trustworthy decentralized virtual platform that sets apart from the crowd, set up on the blockchain, and is possessed by its users.

Who developed the platform?
The Decentraland team has expertise in cryptocurrency, one among many of their projects being the invention of Bitcore (BTX). The leader of the project, Ari Meilich, partnered with technical manager Esteban Ordano.

The advisory board includes:
- ✓ Xiaolai Li (the founder of INBlockchain);
- ✓ Jake Brukhman (the creator of CoinFund);
- ✓ Luis Cuende (the head of the Aragon project);
- ✓ Diego Doval (the former CTO of Ning).

Additionally, Decentraland operates with two other cryptocurrencies, Aragon and District0x.
Currently, there are literally no limits with Decentraland. Using this platform, anything can be created and explored. Users can buy land using the Ethereum blockchain that indisputably confirms ownership.
As a user, you are free to create whatever you desire. Some of the options proposed by the Decentraland team cover live music

shows, casinos, shopping, commercial activities, visits to underwater resorts, and test drives for cars.

All of this takes place in a virtual world with a 360-degree view that can engage users through the web browser or by using a VR visor.

What sets Decentraland apart from other VR platforms?

The most meaningful difference between Decentraland (MANA) and existing VR platforms is its ownership.

The team following the project thinks that public virtual worlds should be managed and governed with open standards. In other words, no central organization should force its will.

In addition to being possessed by users, Decentraland enables them to control the plot of land they own entirely. Also, the owners can derive income from the value generated by other users.

Besides, Decentraland is utterly distinctive from systems where the central organization, which runs the platform, takes a percentage of every transaction. Without a point of centralization, no group can decide on commissions or fees to be paid.

All of this is possible, as mentioned above, through Decentraland's (MANA) use of blockchain technology, which uniquely certifies ownership of a parcel.

How to purchase land?

Buying land is as easy as using MANA, Decentraland's token. Land tiles measure 10 square meters, and there are no limits on vertical buildings; the only constraints are on the base of the constructions. Although, it is relevant to note that Decentraland's earth tiles are sparse. They were especially and purposely designed to increase demand for it and improve the overall user experience and ability to discover its contents.

If the lands were huge, they would never be explored and would also cost very little. Registration for the Terraform Event closed on December 15, 2017.

What is the goal of the MANA token?

MANA is used to purchase lands, either directly from Decentraland or from other users as lands are transferable, and to buy digital goods and services found in the virtual world. The utility of MANA will grow as Decentraland's lands are developed on the Ethereum blockchain. You can buy MANA tokens on leading exchanges. A complete list is available on CoinMarketCap, and they can be stored in an Ethereum wallet.

What are the projects for the future?

The Decentraland project was launched in June 2015, in what they call the Stone Age, when the earth was modeled in the form of a simple grid and pixels were allocated to users by a Proof of Work algorithm. In March 2017, the project set foot in the Bronze Age, and a 3D view was added. Those who purchased MANA, the ERC20 token, were able to get plots of land and then interact with other holders of the same cryptocurrency. Later, the Iron Age added multiplayer support, along with a live chat and avatars.

The last period, the Silicon Age, has opened the world to full VR support.

In March 2018, the group launched the Decentraland Marketplace, a decentralized marketplace, as the name suggests, where you can purchase and sell land belonging to other users.

ETHERLAND
https://etherland.world/

When buying or selling a property, it is essential to have a document that serves as a record and displays all the information that can be found about that land or property. This document, called the cadaster, is used in many countries according to the guidelines established by Napoleon in 1807. However, in other nations, it is not common practice. There, the sale is instead publicly displayed so that it can be verified. This process is an example of decentralization through which it remains challenging to trace sales that are often difficult to prove. This is where Etherland comes in.

Through a worldwide registry known as Estatepedia, Etherland connects real estate units from across the world, allowing people to create, own, and maintain information in an efficiently and transparently. Etherland will empower people to gain control over legal documents, images, terrains data, solar exposure, and more while creating NFTs aimed at developing an entire ecosystem that is a metaverse parallel to that of the Earth. The Etherland platform is an aggregate of interoperable technologies that connect users' digital data with the physical world. It is essentially a decentralized repository that provides free access to information anytime, and from anywhere in the world, for an almost infinite period.
Etherland was created as a solution to the lack of information or its malicious management by the owners. In this way, Etherland binds the owner to their property's information by providing a complete history comprising updates, information, and ownership changes.

The created token is called LAND ID, and on the metaverse, you will have complete control over the property data stored in it, which also be modified. Etherland is the first global Estatepedia running on the Ethereum blockchain that will change the management of land ownership identification, possibly by converting or integrating paper documents into ERC721 tokens and unique IPFS data. The actual owner of the property you wish to digitize can thus have a Verified LAND ID, provided you have sufficient legal information. Since blockchain technology is accepted as legal proof in several countries worldwide, you can get double proof of ownership.

A LAND ID can contain the following information:
- Country
- Type of land
- Type of infrastructure
- City
- Number of issues

For instance, Big Ben has the following identification: GB.LML1, Britain, Landmark, Monument, London, and 1. So far, mainly world monuments have been mined on Etherland.

In addition, the platform has announced the arrival of the application thanks to which users from all over the world will be able to own rare NFTs by capturing them via their smartphones, as a real treasure hunt during which players will be able to secure ownership of these NFTs. Some of those are free and hidden on the map.

MERIDIO
https://www.cofi.tech/

Meridio is another platform based on Ethereum blockchain technology and is dedicated to the fractional ownership of the real estate. It represents one of the thrilling opportunities to create private investments, offering the possibility to reduce and potentially eliminate the various problems of accessibility to real estate investments. The basic idea is that you can own part of a real estate property, for example, a building with offices inside or a store in a trendy neighborhood. With Meridio, you can own a part of that building and do so more easily, a method that also allows investors to resell the fractional property and get instant liquidity quickly. The blockchain substantially reduces the cost of a transaction. It will enable you to finance the property transparently because this asset offers all the metadata essential to choose the best property based on your expectations.

Therefore, Meridio aims to provide transparency and clear information to make the real estate market more liquid, accessible, and efficient for different levels of investors, from individuals to large companies. Its founders, Mo Shaikh and Corbin Page, started exploring the various possibilities that blockchain could offer until they decided to put their ideas together and found Meridio. As far as investors are concerned, Meridio offers several advantages:

1. It doesn't require a minimum investment or seed capital;
2. It reduces transaction costs, which occur in peer-to-peer and direct;

3. It develops the liquidity of the portfolio by allowing shares or bonds to be relocated.

On the other hand, once ownership of a property on Meridio has been obtained, it is possible to:

1. Unlock additional capital;
2. Streamline transaction processes through smart contracts;
3. Analyze asset-specific data in real-time.

The blockchain industry is moving beyond speculation. With platforms like Meridio, it is entering the era of utility and getting a substantial idea of real estate's future. Meridio runs on ConsenSys, the platform founded by Joseph Lubin, in New York, that operates on the Ethereum blockchain. The integrated stable coin is Maker's DAI. Using a stable coin allows for the benefits of having smart contracts included in trustless transactions and virtually instant timing while avoiding the volatility of cryptocurrency.

In addition, users can purchase or exchange tokens in the app directly with DAI in a direct, trustless exchange between tokens and DAI, meaning the transaction can happen without an escrow service and without being subject to unspecified price volatility.

Meridio has integrated the Airswap widget into users' wallets so they can quickly convert any Ether they hold in Metamask to DAI. The wallet page provides each user with the DAI and ETH balance of their linked wallet so that they can quickly see their current position and convert currencies accordingly.

OVR
https://www.ovr.ai/

I t is safe to say that as of 2020, the real estate market has seen a new boom in the virtual land sector. It has indeed seen a substantial increase in supply and demand. Perhaps also due to the pandemic, there has been a greater attraction to virtual lands, which many investors have purchased.

Virtual lands are in great demand for various reasons, the first of all being profit:

• On virtual lands, it is possible to place structures and create real virtual galleries containing crypto artworks.
• You can rent and sell.
• You may host crypto games. A booming universe of possibilities is feasible thanks to blockchain technology.
• You get to decide in full autonomy the type of experience that the user can live.

In this context, OVR, an open-source augmented reality platform built on the Ethereum blockchain that provides users with virtual experiences inside a virtual land called OVRLand, is positioned in full relief. OVR recently became known because of a disruptive piece of news: until April 30, 2021, it was possible to purchase the Eiffel Tower in the form of NFT tokens with an auction base of $7,400. Overall, OVR has sold over 200,000 NFTs from its OVRLand in the four months since its launch, and on April 27, in collaboration with artists Giovanni Motta, Marco Biscardi, and Rok Bogataj, it opened an art gallery that reached 7,000 views in just a few hours.

The new real-time digital experience is made possible on your smartphone or camera. The OVR app is available on both Android and Apple stores. It allows users with a mobile device or smart glass to enjoy personalized, interactive augmented reality experiences in the real world. It can be defined as a new standard in augmented reality, where geographic experiences are based on the user's location.

With OVR's augmented reality, everything is becoming possible, even partying together. Each user has their own 3D avatar, which can interact with other users' avatars and participate in live performances. These experiences are available in augmented reality with more original scenery, lighting effects, and animals of all kinds, all within your own home, which you can completely transform. OVR is the brainchild of Italian CEO Davide Cuttini. OVR has operational headquarters in Italy, precisely in Udine, while the platform sees its international headquarters in Estonia.

The OVR ecosystem is supported by a grid of hexagons covering the Earth's entire surface, called "Over the Planet." The hexagons, called OVRLands, have a specific geographic location and a standard size of 300 square meters. ERC-721 tokens allow for decentralized ownership of the resource and experiences within it. OVRLand can be divided into multiple hexagons that allow for more precise localization within the possession. This means that owners who have invested in a land will be able to decide in full autonomy what kind of experience the user may have once inside. These OVRLands can be traded freely between users in a decentralized way through the OVR Owner marketplace. Thus, as on any decentralized platform, the community has complete control over OVRLands and OVR Experiences.

Economic incentives, development, and growth are all possible for Land asset owners in OVRs, precisely because of the blockchain technology, which makes the scarce and unique asset controllable by the owner alone. To purchase OVRLands, one must own a metamask wallet. The land can be chosen at will by bidding to purchase it. The programming is user-friendly and potentially open to any activity. For example, an artist can buy a gallery in which to display and sell his crypto artworks or charge an entrance fee, rent, and much more.

You can also stake the OVR token in three different ways:
- A 5% annual interest with no strings attached to the amount of tokens.
- A 15% interest for a 10-month block.
- Rewards for solving blockchain nodes.

The possible investments on OVR are infinite. It is a fertile ground for exciting ideas and projects in uninterrupted growth and with a considerable opportunity to make a profit. A project certainly to be monitored and in which it is worth considering investing.

REPUBLIC REALM
https://www.republicrealm.com/

Republic Realm is an online investment platform that saw the light in 2016 thanks to the collaboration of the two founders, Ken Nguyen and Bryant Mint. Headquartered in New York and San Francisco, the company's office network expands to Moscow, Shanghai, and Tel Aviv. The platform has investors from all over the world, among which are some of the giants in the industry, such as:

- Binance;
- Passport Capital;
- Tribe Capital;
- Zhen Fund;
- Venture Capital, and private investors.

What Republic Realm offers is a unique investment opportunity in real estate. Through the platform, investors will be equipped to interact on all metaverse existing today, and will then be able to:

✓ Acquire.
✓ Manage.
✓ Develop. Applying the principles of real-world development, the platform aims to create memorable spaces that are points of attraction and focus on the various metaverses that increase interaction possibilities.
✓ Buy and sell virtual land.

Where? On metaverses ranging from Decentraland to Axie Infinity via The Sandbox, Cryptovoxels, Somnium Space, and many more. Creating, publishing, and monetizing through NFTs will then be possible on multiple parallel digital universes through a single decentralized platform. This investment fund focuses on exclusivity, and thus, limits access to only 99 accredited investors and by invitation only.

Republic Realm's focal point is to create the intersection between the technological possibilities of virtual reality and blockchain. Being an investment ground with no real boundaries, that is extraordinarily malleable and will allow brands, companies, and investors from all over the world to seize a unique opportunity, the most avant-garde brands find in the metaverse the possibility to stimulate a whole new customer engagement. Musicians and crypto artists, gaming, lifestyle, and hospitality companies, as well as fashion and consumer brands are just some of the main targets that can invest in this platform.

After seeing what the investment opportunities are and the doors they open, we need to understand how to access them. As mentioned above, you can only enter this platform only by invitation. To try to be invited into this fund, you will need to fill out the information form available on the website, answer some concrete questions that will take into account your accreditations as an investor, the maximum capital you intend to invest, and a brief presentation of your project. After completing this process, the Republic Realm team will consider your application, and you will then receive feedback via email.

SOMNIUM SPACE
https://somniumspace.com/

S omnium Space is an open-source blockchain-based VR world within which you can tokenize your own custom VR avatars. This virtual world is characterized by a social one. Within this world, you can, in fact:

- Play and relax with many games;
- Socialize with other avatars;
- Visit places and live virtual experiences;
- Rent or buy apartments, houses, or lands;
- Have fun going to the movies, on rides, at the zoo, and much more.

No only a blockchain-based virtual game, Somnium Space is the world's first virtual world with equity crowdfunding. It is a new and unique game shaped by players who can meet, socialize, participate in events together, and monetize. Somnium Space's CEO and founder, Artur Sychov, worked for years as an investment trader before becoming a serial entrepreneur and has always firmly believed in the future of virtual worlds to develop human interaction. So, in 2007, along with his able-bodied team, Sychov created a platform that aims to allow users to explore the virtual world. Through this decentralized blockchain platform, users can model augmented reality to choose to buy or sell land, participate in events, or organize them. Somnium Space is a fully interconnected world accessible from any device, even in 2D.

However, the ownership of the virtual land is always at the base of the economy of virtual reality. Within your own land, it is, in fact, possible to do anything, and the game allows you to buy three types of lands:

1. A small parcel, which is equivalent to 10 meters in vertical and horizontal limits;
2. A medium parcel that is 25 meters high and wide;
3. A large parcel that is 50 meters in upper development as well.

Each terrain can be increased, and additional resources can be purchased directly from the store. The customization possibilities are unlimited, and after building on your land, you can sell the result and monetize it if you wish to. On The Builder, the software that allows you to create on the properties, the only limit is your imagination. On the one hand, the blockchain enables the ownership of lands and assets, but on the other hand, it is possible to adjust one's layout configuration, record information regarding one's avatar, build anything the user wants, program one's experience, and monetize through it.

Somnium Space is an entirely immersive world in which the weather changes daily; if it's sunny, the buildings created by the users cast their shadows on the environment. All of this serves to awaken the body's senses and fuel the bond between the avatars. Users can actually own the land, just like in the real world. Using blockchain as its backbone, Somnium Space enables users to purchase plots of land, on which they can build whatever they want. And just like in real life, downtown land is more expensive because of its inherent appeal. In addition, the team developed a fully functioning world loaded with events, encounters, and places to explore. People can enjoy live concerts, educational conferences, and sports competitions, or just sit in the park and watch the birds fly by.The virtual currency within this world is called Cube. Any NFT can be used within the platform and placed in the gallery, for example, thus allowing anyone to monetize their creations instantly. Somnium Space is one of those platforms that have allowed the virtual real estate sector to make that quantum leap and enter rightfully among the first choices of investors and entrepreneurs from around the world.

SUPERWORLD
https://www.superworldapp.com/

The platform, launched in 2017, was founded by Hrish Lotlikar and Max Woon, and uses the ERC-721 standard. Users who purchase land on SuperWorld own a non-fungible token with multiple monetization possibilities, including the opportunities to:

- ✓ Create virtual games.
- ✓ Open stores and e-commerce.
- ✓ Sell land.
- ✓ Create an augmented reality meeting place.
- ✓ Create exhibitions of artwork.

All the investment possibilities on a real plot of land seem potentially replicable on a digital plot of land in this metaverse. Properties not yet purchased on the platform have a base price of 0.1 ETH. They can be accessed by logging into SuperWorld and creating a wallet such as Metamask, Portis, or Fortmatic, and uploading Ethereum currency to it.

SuperWorld is one of the most notable metaverses within the NFT world and one of the most desirable for investors in digital real estate, with 64.8 billion virtual land parcels geographically mapped to the Earth. The entire globe has been mapped on the platform and is divided into 100 x 100 m polygonal real estate plots and put up for sale.

Today, a single stretch of Manhattan's High Line sells for over 333 ETH. The platform allows its users to own a unique piece of planet Earth and customize it according to their preferences, from augmented reality to 3D animations to audio, video, and text installations. This augmented reality will be visible not only by visiting SuperWorld but also by all those who, owning the specific app, will frame a particular place with their cellphones' cameras or VR glasses. In addition to the land, the platform offers endless opportunities to earn money through various initiatives, such as:

• NFT Saloon. There, NFT creators of all kinds can showcase and sell their creations: video games, crypto art, collectibles, music, and any other possible combination.
• Artist Resident. The goal is the creation of a living artistic community. That is why there is a list of resident artists, the best NFT artists owning properties, and land on the platform.
• SuperWorld Star Chamber. This is a virtual gallery where the platform showcases some of the most admired and appreciated non-fungible-token creators.

Investors and advisers include DraperGorenHolm, SOSV, CapitalFactory, Stephen Wolfram (creator of Mathematica and Wolfram Alpha), Bob Metcalfe (inventor of Ethernet and Metcalfe's Law), Richard Ling (founder of Rembrandt Ventures), Bob Fabbio (CEO of Tivoli), Robert Scoble (author, futurist), Mariana Danilovic, (founder of Infiom and Hollywood Portfolio), Phil Rowley (head of futures at Omnicom Group), Nitin Gaur (head of digital assets at IBM), Tobias Ratschiller (CEO of CryptoCoinNews), Chris Thomas (head of digital assets at Swissquote Bank), William Burns (a pioneer of the metaverse), Brian Thorp (CEO of Wealthtender), and Joseph Chan (managing partner of Guardian Property Advisors).

THE SANDBOX
https://www.sandbox.game/en/

The Sandbox is the digital land buying and selling game on the blockchain, a set of products and services to create, manage, and enjoy various adventures and experiences. What happens when blockchain, gaming, and real estate come together? Several experiments have been conducted over the years, but little has been discussed, and nothing has reached the broad public yet. However, this time around, that could change: with the NFT craze filling the pages of the newspapers and business blogs, a project — more than three years in development — is about to come within everyone's reach.

The Sandbox is a game about blockchain. It is its simplest definition, but it also is the one that makes less justice to the complexity of this project, which could impact the virtual real estate industry. Nowadays, The Sandbox is reaching its peak of notoriety and success. The platform is a set of products and services to create, manage, and enjoy experiences and adventures using the blockchain as a permanent ledger to give value and uniqueness to creation.

It's difficult to describe everything that can be done on The Sandbox. A few months ago, after a three-year development, the platform offered its first product, a map composed of 166,464 digital land plots which has been sold on multiple occasions. Now, the map is 45% complete, but there already are interesting economic dynamics that make one piece of land more meaningful than another. In general, the value of all the lots is increasing every day because the map has been fixed: when the lots to buy are finished, you can do nothing but rent them or use them for playing, among other things.

Lots have been put up for sale directly on the website or are available for investment through an auction system on Opensea, one of the best-known NFT exchange platforms.

For example, in February alone, more than $2.8 million in lots were sold, and a single piece of land was auctioned for about $300,000. Those who purchase at such high prices do so for a single reason: some lots have strategic importance on the map. Some of the most influential buyers, in fact, are fundamental entities both in and outside of the crypto world. For instance, the video game and console manufacturer Atari bought lots for as much as $2 million. Meanwhile, Coinmarketcap (a data aggregator on all crypto) and Binance (the biggest exchange marketplace for crypto volumes in the world) both bought many lots, and this shows: it's all written on the blockchain.

Owning a lot close to a major brand means being capable to offer that lot to third-party customers by telling them about the proximity to products and services that everyone uses, precisely like when a real estate agent tries to convince someone to buy an apartment in downtown Rome rather than in the suburbs or in a small town many miles away. In both cases, proximity to services (whether physical or digital) makes a difference. Indeed, because lots are not just pieces of land, like in Monopoly or the real world, you can build on them and construct a building with facilities and scenes that are suitable for one experience or another. For instance, Atari could create a colossal game with all the lots they got. At the same time, a developer could build a conference room to rent to communities and businesses that want to host events in distinctive scenarios.

On the one hand, there are the users of the world, and on the other hand, there are the creators. The latter, through a software package provided by The Sandbox, can both create games (with

Game Maker) and design objects and characters (with VoxEdit), which they can then resell on the trading platform, available in beta version since March 30. In both circumstances, creators are digital artisans providing the elements or experiences that make The Sandbox a metaverse in its own right.

During this time of significant growth, the platform team has put together several initiatives to fund creators' work. At the launch of the beta platform, 46 artists had produced 112 creations, which can be added to their lands. Everything created is not owned by The Sandbox, but credited directly to the creator and recorded on the blockchain, thus allowing them to retain copyright.

The Sandbox is a reasonable example of the complexity that an application on the blockchain can achieve and how decentralization can be leveraged to redistribute wealth. The application is accessible via the Ethereum blockchain, which has been the star of a noteworthy increase in transaction volume over the past six months, leading to increased fees per transaction.

CRYPTO DUKEDOM
To know us a little more
We believe in the crypto world.
Our goal is to make it accessible to all people.
For us, this is the future.
Or rather, the future that is already becoming present.
There are new fantastic worlds, full of opportunities.
There are difficulties, problems to be solved.
As in all things, we know it.
Thousands of people are working to solve them and constantly create new possibilities. Even now.
We do our part by investing, sharing, and creating value for those like us who have approached all this inspired.
Thank you so much for choosing us!

Your satisfaction matters to us!
Did you like this book? Did you find it interesting and helpful?
Is there anything you care about that we didn't cover?
We are always looking for ways to improve.
The topic is evolving so fast that we are committed to periodically improving our content.

Feel free to contact us at cryptodukedom@gmail.com
You trusted us. Your opinion is valuable to us.
And kindly leave us a review. It makes the difference.

We wish you the best.
Crypto Dukedom.

Environmental awareness is important to us.

This book is printed-on-demand to reduce excess production. The ink is chlorine-free, and the acid-free interior paper stock is provided by a supplier certified by the Forest Stewardship Council.

We chose to print in black and white on cream-colored paper made with 30% post-consumer recycled material.

We choose minimalism and try to select the essential.

We believe you appreciate and share our choices.

We trust that you, together with us, will continue to revise your daily practices to make sure we are doing our part to protect the environment.

Printed in Great Britain
by Amazon